What the
Constitution
Says

THE FIRST AMENDMENT:

"Congress shall make no law . . . abridging
the freedom of speech or of the press. . . ."

THE FIFTH AMENDMENT:

"No person shall be held to answer for
a capital, or otherwise infamous crime . . .
nor be deprived of life, liberty or property,
without due process of law. . . ."

THE SIXTH AMENDMENT:

"In all criminal prosecutions, the accused
shall enjoy the right to a speedy and
public trial, by an impartial jury. . . ."

THE FOURTEENTH AMENDMENT:

"No State . . . shall deprive any person of life,
liberty or property, without due process of law. . . ."

Free Press v. Fair Trial

TELEVISION AND OTHER MEDIA IN THE COURTROOM

BY MICHAEL KRONENWETTER

FRANKLIN WATTS 1986 AN IMPACT BOOK
NEW YORK LONDON TORONTO SYDNEY

Library of Congress Cataloging in Publication Data

Kronenwetter, Michael.
Free press v. fair trial.

(An Impact book)
Bibliography: p.
Includes index.
Summary: Surveys the debate over whether radio,
television, and other media in the courtroom interfere
with a defendant's rights to a fair trial.
1. Conduct of court proceedings—United States—
Juvenile literature. 2. Video tapes in courtroom
proceedings—United States—Juvenile literature.
3. Free press and fair trial—United States—Juvenile
literature. 4. Television broadcasting of news—United
States—Juvenile literature. [1. Free press and fair
trial. 2. Video tapes in courtroom proceedings.
3. Conduct of court proceedings] I. Title. II. Title:
Free press versus fair trial.
KF8725.Z9K76 1986   345.73′056   85-25386
      ISBN 0-531-10153-3   347.30556

Contents

Free Press
v.
Fair Trial

Introduction

The relationship between America's news media and its courts has always been a special one. It is different from the comparable relationship of the press and the courts anywhere else. It is most different of all from those relationships in the totalitarian countries of the world—both those of the political right and the political left. In such countries, all institutions, including both the press and the courts, are expected to serve the government in power. The press is used as a propaganda tool of the government, telling the people only what the government wants them to hear, while the courts are used to repress opposition to the government.

In the United States, things were designed very differently. Here, as elsewhere, the courts are an arm of the government, but they are set up to be independent of the other branches of government, the executive and the legislative. Instead of being intended to act as agents of repression, under our Constitution the courts have been given the responsibility of protecting the rights of the people against any effort to repress these rights.

The press, for its part, is not an arm of the government at all. Far from being a propaganda tool of the government, the American press has a long tradition, dating from before the American revolution, of criticizing the government and exposing its mistakes and abuses. What's more, that tradition is protected by the Constitution itself, which guarantees the press's independence from government control.

In totalitarian countries there is little reason for tensions between the press and the courts. Both institutions, after all, serve the same master—the government in power. In the United States, however, such tensions sometimes arise. They are, in fact, built into a system in which each of the two great institutions must to some extent serve as a watchdog on the other.

The courts, however independent they may be from the other branches of government, are still an arm of government themselves. As such, they are subject to the scrutiny of the press, and to its criticism. The courts, meanwhile, have the job not only of protecting the rights of the press (even to criticize them) but also of protecting the rights of others from violation by the press.

It has been said that few people like to be criticized, and that no institutions do. This is as true of both the press and the courts as it is of anyone else. Consequently, their relationship is a complex and often a very difficult one. They are at once allies and adversaries—allies in the ongoing task of preserving America's freedoms, adversaries when their differing responsibilities in carrying out that task come into conflict.

One area in which those differing responsibilities have come into dramatic conflict is that of modern journalistic technology—cameras and microphones, and the ability to broadcast the sights and sounds of the courtroom to people all across the country. The ability to photograph court proceedings and even to broadcast them has been available for decades, but the question of whether the media ought to be able to use that ability is still a matter of heated debate. This book will examine both sides of that debate, focusing, finally, on the questions raised by the televising of criminal trials.

These are far from the only questions raised by the relationship between modern media technology and the courts, but they are ones which have raised the most public interest, and the most controversy. It is in the criminal courts where the drama of the law, and of those individuals who come into conflict with it, is played out most starkly. And it is the televising of criminal trials which brings, or seems to bring, two of our most important constitutional rights—the right to a fair trial and the right to a free press—into sharpest conflict.

In order to understand the importance of this conflict and of the controversy that surrounds it, it is necessary to understand something of these two great institutions, the press and the courts, and of the fundamental rights they represent.

1

The Courts
v.
The Press

THE JOB OF THE COURTS

There are several different kinds and levels of courts in the United States. Some correspond to the different branches of government. These include municipal (or city) courts, county courts, state courts, and federal courts, all the way up to the Supreme Court of the United States. Specialized courts deal with specific kinds of cases. There are divorce courts, for example, as well as traffic courts, small claims courts, and courts that do nothing but handle appeals from the decisions of other courts.

The basic function of all these courts can be stated very simply: It is to resolve disputes.

But that simple statement masks an extremely complicated reality. Just as there are many kinds of courts, those courts are called upon to resolve many kinds of disputes. Some disputes are between private individuals, as when one person sues another for breaking a contract. Other disputes may be between a branch of government and a private person, as when a citizen is sued for under-payment of taxes, or when an individual sues the government for violation of his or her rights. Still other disputes may be between governments—the government of a state, for example, and the federal government—or even between different agencies of the same level of government.

Many disputes have to do with business matters, particularly with the interpretation of contracts. Some have to do with public questions, such as the application of the Constitution or of lesser laws. Another large category of disputes consists of criminal matters, cases in which the government of a particular state, or the federal government, accuses an individual of committing a crime. (It is this last kind of dispute with which we are primarily concerned in this book.)

Whatever the level of the court, and whatever the kind of dispute, the primary effort of the American judicial system is to be fair. "Fairness," as Justice Potter Stewart of the United States Supreme Court once said, "is what justice really is."

In part, this effort to be fair is simply an attempt to deal evenly with the people whose disputes come before the courts. Clearly it would be wrong for the court—a branch of government—to favor one citizen unfairly over another. Even more clearly, it would be wrong to convict an innocent person of a crime.

But the need to be fair is far more than a desire to deal evenly with the individuals who happen to appear in court. It is essential for the social and political health of the entire society.

The courts are a key element in the relationship between the government and the people. The courts are the places in which the government endeavors to settle for its citizens those disputes the citizens are unable to settle for themselves; and the places in which the laws protecting the citizens are ultimately enforced. It is, then, absolutely vital that the people have faith in the essential fairness of the courts.

Only when the courts are fair—and are *recognized* as being fair—can the people have faith in their ability to resolve disputes. To put it another way, only when the courts are fair can people have faith that their government will deal fairly with *them*. And that elementary faith is crucial if the social system under which we live is to hold together. Without it, people would lose faith not only in the government but in each other. Having no trust in the law, they would increasingly take the law into their own hands. In many countries, at many different times in history, such lawlessness has been followed by anarchy—and anarchy, all too often, has been followed by dictatorship and tyranny. Under such totalitarian governments, of course, the ideal of a fair trial becomes a mockery, as the courts become little more than an instrument for repression.

The importance of a fair trial, then, goes far beyond the importance of any given court case, even beyond the importance of the judicial system as a whole. As Arthur L. Goodhart, the British legal historian, has pointed out: "The establishment of the modern dictatorships was not the result of a failure of democracy; it was due to a failure of law." Consequently he has argued (and few legal scholars would disagree with him) that fair trials are not just desirable for their own sakes, they are "essential . . . to civilization" itself.

DUE PROCESS OF LAW

The framers of the Constitution knew as well as anyone the vital importance of fair trials, and yet the term "fair trial" does not appear in the Constitution. Instead the Constitution as originally passed guaranteed only the right of citizens to be tried by a jury. Even the first nine amendments to the Constitution—the Bill of Rights—

speak in terms not of "fair trial," but of "due process of law."

Although this may seem strange, it is actually quite logical. A fair trial is the goal. Due process of law—a system of rules of procedure that can be evenly applied to all parties—is the best means of reaching that goal.

The Constitution left the question of what those specific rules should be largely unsettled. With a few exceptions (like the right to a jury), due process was to be determined by the Congress (for trials in the federal courts) and by the various state legislatures (for trials in the lesser courts), and by the common law, all as interpreted by the courts.

The original states had all been British colonies. Their social and political traditions were inherited from England, and so were their concepts of due process of law. The rules of procedure they established were largely adopted (and adapted) from British models.

An American trial, like its British counterpart, is an adversary proceeding. That is, it is a kind of contest between two opponents. One side (called the prosecution in criminal cases and the plaintiff in other cases) makes an accusation against the other side (called the defense). The accusing side goes first, laying out the strongest case it can, within the rules of procedure, against the defendant. Then the defense gets its chance to refute the accuser's claims.

Both sides proceed by presenting arguments, as well as witnesses and other evidence, in support of their positions. Over the years, elaborate rules have evolved governing just what kinds of arguments, testimony, and other evidence can be permitted in a trial. These rules are subject to change over time as more experience is gained by the courts and as conditions change, both in the courts themselves and in society at large. For the most part, the changes in these rules have tended to provide greater protections for citizens in their dealings with the government and greater protections for those accused of crimes. These rules form an important part of the due process guaranteed by the Constitution.

Once both sides have made their cases, a decision is made in favor of one side or another. That decision is made by a third party, or parties, who have no direct personal interest in the question in dispute. In noncriminal cases, the decision is usually made by a judge. In some criminal cases (as well as in some noncriminal cases) in which the defendant so chooses, it is made by a jury.

That jury consists of "peers" of the defendant. (That term has usually been interpreted to mean simply ordinary people, chosen from the community at large.) They are expected to make their decision solely on the basis of the arguments and evidence presented to them in court. That rule is necessary because only what takes place in court is controlled by the rules of procedure, the rules designed to assure fairness to both sides.

It is extremely important to the process that the jury be, in the word used by the Constitution, "impartial." One major element of that impartiality is that the members of the jury come into the courtroom with open minds, unprejudiced either for or against either side in the dispute.

This is one area in which the courts and the press have sometimes come into conflict. Obviously, the more pretrial publicity there has been about a case, the harder it will be for the court to find people to serve on the jury who have not already been prejudiced by that publicity. And even after a case has come to trial, the jurors may be influenced by press coverage.

Judges have attempted to counteract this prejudicial influence in many ways. Jurors are instructed not to read press accounts of the trial and not to watch television news or listen to radio reports, until the trial is over. But in the modern age, when the press, radio and television seem to be everywhere in our lives, that is a difficult instruction for many people to follow. What's more, it is impossible for a judge (or the defense) to be really sure if the jurors have even seriously attempted to follow it. In some cases, where the judge is deeply concerned about the possibility of press coverage influencing the jury, the jury has been sequestered. That is, they have been kept confined, usually in a comfortable hotel, away from all possibility of contamination by press coverage, until their verdict has been reached.

In extreme cases in the past, judges have resorted to the drastic step of issuing gag orders. These were orders forbidding the press to report on certain aspects of a criminal case. Sometimes they forbade reporting on a particular case at all.

In such instances, the judge had decided that the defendant's right to a fair trial would be jeopardized by press coverage, and that the defendant's right overrode the press's right to publish information about the case.

This form of press censorship became very popular among certain elements of the judiciary in the 1970s. Gag orders threatened to become a common feature of the press/court relationship, and the press was becoming increasingly concerned. When the issue finally reached the Supreme Court, the Court decided in favor of the press. It ruled that gag orders were almost always an inappropriate method of defending the right to a fair trial, and that, except in the most extreme cases, they were an unconstitutional infringement of the right of freedom of the press.

The need for the jury to be impartial does not begin and end at the courtroom door. The jury is expected to hear the entire case presented by both sides in the dispute, and then to weigh all the evidence and arguments carefully before reaching its decision. This obligation implies several requirements, among them that the jurors be present throughout the trial, and that they be attentive and take their duty seriously. It also implies that the trial should be conducted in an atmosphere conducive to calm deliberation on the part of the jury.

It is up to the trial judge to assure the jury this kind of judicial atmosphere. To that end, the judge has certain powers and obligations to control the behavior of everyone in his or her courtroom. This includes not just the parties to the dispute, their attorneys, and witnesses, but also any spectators who might be present—including the representatives of the press.

The Sixth Amendment to the Constitution guarantees all defendants in the federal courts the right to a "public trial." (The Fourteenth Amendment later extended this right, along with others, to the state courts as well.) This right implies the right of spectators to be present at trials. It has also been generally interpreted to imply the right of at least some members of the press to be present as well. It is only through their presence that the public at large can be informed of the trial proceedings.

The public and the press are there to assure the defendant a fair trial. They are there to act as a check on unscrupulous judges, prosecutors or juries who might "railroad" an innocent person. They are there to—literally—*see* that justice is done. Consequently, their right to be present does *not* imply a right to behave in any way that would interfere with the process of justice.

Clearly the jury cannot be expected to decide a case impartially if it is faced with constant demonstrations by spectators for or against a defendant. Equally clearly, neither the jury nor the witnesses nor anyone else involved in the trial can be expected to do their duties properly if they are faced with distracting and disruptive behavior on the part of spectators.

It is the judge's responsibility to see that such things do not take place in the courtroom. As we shall see in chapter 2, it was this responsibility which first brought judges into conflict with the press over the use of such journalistic technologies as photography and broadcasting in the courtroom.

FREEDOM OF THE PRESS

The other great right at issue in the controversy over the use of modern journalistic technology in the courtroom is that of freedom of the press. Along with freedom of religion and freedom of speech, freedom of the press was placed right at the top of the Bill of Rights. The very First Amendment to the Constitution requires that Congress make no law "abridging . . . the freedom of the press."

When the framers of the Bill of Rights enshrined press freedom in the First Amendment, they were taking a radical step. No other government on earth then guaranteed the press such freedom, and none ever had. If one wanted to find the reason why other governments were reluctant to grant the press free reign, one had to look no farther than the recent experience of the American Revolution itself. The press in the American colonies had been an effective weapon against the British colonial governments. The writings of such journalists as Thomas Paine had helped to bring on the American Revolution, and once the revolution had started, they had helped to spur it to success. No other government wanted to guarantee the freedom of a press that might use that freedom to bring the government down.

The new government of the United States, however, did just that. Its founders were determined to start not just a new country, but a new *kind* of country. It was to be a country without a monarch, a representational democracy, a country in which power proceeded from the people and in which the people chose their own leaders. In that kind of country a free press was not just an affordable luxury, it was a necessity.

If the people were to choose their leaders, and then to decide from time to time whether to keep them or throw them out, the people had to know what their leaders were doing. Information about the government and its leaders had to be free to circulate among the public, and the only feasible medium for that was the printed word, the press. The United States of 1790 was nowhere near as large as the United States of today, but it was much too large for word of mouth to be counted on to spread the news.

The press served another vital function besides that of disseminating the news. It was also a vehicle for political debate, another absolute necessity in a democracy.

In order to exercise these functions, it was necessary that the press be kept out of government control. If the government could regulate the press, it was feared, the press would end up like that in totalitarian countries, telling the people only what the government wanted them to know. It would print information flattering to the government and the people who ran the government and withhold any information damaging to them. The only point of view that could be widely expressed in print would be the point of view of the faction in power, the faction that controlled the press.

On the other hand, if the press could print whatever it wanted, information flattering to the government or damning to it, ideas supporting the government or opposing it, then the people would have a wide range of information and ideas to choose from. They could make up their own minds. As Thomas Jefferson put it, "When the press is free and every man able to read, all is safe."

It is important to recognize that the founders of our country did not assume that the press, granted freedom, would always tell the truth. Far from it. Thomas Jefferson himself wrote to a friend that "Advertisements contain the only truth to be relied on in a newspaper." And although he was overstating the case even then, newspapers in those days were clearly less reliable than they are today. Most of them made no effort to be objective—or even to *appear* to be objective—at all. They were wholeheartedly partisan, praising their political friends to the

[15]

skies and berating their enemies mercilessly. But even so, the founders felt that the newspapers' freedom was an essential element of the free society they intended to build. As the French visitor to America, Alexis de Tocqueville, explained in his study *Democracy in America,* "In order to enjoy the inestimable benefits that the liberty of the press ensures, it is necessary to submit to the inevitable evils that it creates." The most important of those "inestimable benefits" is the free flow of information and ideas, a flow vital to the functioning of the democratic process.

The freedom of the press, then, is not a special privilege given to a handful of journalists as a kind of favor to them. Rather, it is a right given to ensure the freedom, not primarily of journalists, but of society as a whole. The freedom of the press and the freedom of the people are inseparable. As the twentieth-century Supreme Court justice George Sutherland expressed the relationship: "To allow [the press] to be fettered is to be fettered ourselves." And as another twentieth-century justice, Felix Frankfurter, said, "Freedom of the press is not an end in itself but a means to the end of a free society."

HISTORY OF FREEDOM OF THE PRESS

Freedom of the press was not a new idea when the United States of America originally guaranteed it in the First Amendment to the Constitution. But, in historical terms at least, it was not a very old idea either.

Like many other principles of American political philosophy, it came to this country by way of England. The first great argument in favor of freedom of the press was written in that country in 1644 by the poet John Milton. Called the *Areopagitica,* Milton's document helped to bring an end to the practice of licensing the press in England, a device by which the British Parliament had kept the press under its control.

Even after licensing was abolished, the press in Britain was far from free. The so-called "law of seditious libel" virtually forbade the press to criticize the government. The concept was a sweeping one. Libel was defined as any malicious published attack, and sedition as any act that tended to stir up hostility or even resistance to the government. Seditious libel, then, was interpreted to mean any published attack on the government or its leaders, whether the charges made were true or not. True charges against the government, in fact, were considered to be even more seditious than false ones. The government reasoned that true charges, since they expressed a real grievance, were likely to stir up even more hostility than false charges.

The same principle of seditious libel was applied in Britain's American colonies in the eighteenth century, although it seems to have been less readily accepted here. In a famous case, a German immigrant printer named John Peter Zenger was arrested for publishing seditious libels against the governor of New York in 1735. Zenger's attorney argued that such a concept was wrong, that "truth ought to govern" in the matter of libel, and that the press should not be blamed for printing the truth no matter how damaging that truth might be to the government. This notion was eagerly accepted by the New York jury, which took only a few minutes to declare Zenger innocent. The verdict was widely applauded. Already, several decades before the Revolution, freedom of the press was a popular idea in America.

Even after the Revolution, however, and after the First Amendment was passed guaranteeing that Congress would "make no law . . . abridging . . . the freedom of the press," the government found it tempting to do just that. In 1798, the Congress, which was controlled by members of the Federalist Party, passed the Alien and Sedition Acts, which were designed to muzzle criticism of the government by that part of the press that was sympathetic to Thomas Jefferson's Republican Party. The commitment to press freedoms was already deeply ingrained in the American consciousness, however, and public outcry managed to halt enforcement of the Acts within a short time.

Throughout most of the nineteenth century, the press in the United States enjoyed a freedom unparalleled in history. Newspapers felt free to attack government leaders unmercifully. President Lincoln, himself, was called a traitor in several newspapers without anything being done to silence them.

The same spirit of unrestrained criticism characterized the press's coverage of trials during that period. In later years, courts would become seriously concerned that press treatment of criminal cases might violate defendants' rights by inflaming public opinion against them. For much of the nineteenth century, however, the press felt free to attack and vilify criminal defendants in ways that would never even be considered today. It was common for accused persons to be referred to in the press as "madmen" or "curs"; and for papers to editorialize even before trials began that the defendants were clearly guilty, and that it would be better for the community if they were simply taken out and hanged.

The Fourteenth Amendment to the Constitution was passed in 1868. It declared, among other things, that "[n]o State shall make or enforce any law which shall abridge the privileges or immunities of citizens of the United States, nor shall any State deprive any person of life, liberty or property, without due process of law; nor deny to any person within its jurisdiction the equal protection of the laws."

Designed to deal with the political aftermath of the Civil War, and particularly with the status of the freed slaves, the Fourteenth Amendment was at first interpreted quite narrowly by the courts. Eventually, however, it would have far-reaching consequences both for the right to freedom of the press and the right to a fair trial. Its ultimate effect was to extend the federal guarantees of the First Amendment and of "due process" to the states.

For the first several decades of its existence, though, the Fourteenth Amendment did little to enhance freedom of the press. But then, press freedom was not seriously threatened during that time.

America's entry into World War I did bring about such a threat. The government's urge to censor the press is always strongest during wartime, and it was strongest of all during World War I. This fact had to do with the large number of German immigrants in the United States at that time. Fearing this large population of alleged potential enemies within America's borders, Congress first passed the Espionage Act of 1917 and then the Sedition Act of 1918. These acts constituted the broadest attempt to censor the press in this country since the Alien and Sedition Acts of 1798. They limited not only the pro-German press (and there was some) but the many German-language papers that served the immigrant community, and all publications that favored either pacifism or socialism as well.

In 1919, the year after the war ended, a landmark case reached the Supreme Court which tested the government's power to censor the press. Although the conviction of a particular newspaper was upheld, the decision increased the freedom of the press in general. The Court's decision, written by Chief Justice Oliver Wendell Holmes, declared: "the question . . . is whether the words [to be censored] are used in such circumstances and are of such a nature as to create a clear and present danger" to the country. While this "clear and present danger" rule did not forbid government censorship altogether, it did greatly limit the power of the government to repress the publication of unpopular political ideas.

When World War II came along, a different kind of censorship was imposed. This time it was accomplished without any new Alien and Sedition Acts. Instead, it was self-imposed by the media. They did it partly to help with the war effort and partly to prevent forced censorship by the government.

During the 1950s, a great fear of communism swept the United States. A number of politicians and other opinion leaders, led by Senator Joseph McCarthy of Wisconsin, convinced many Americans that communist spies had infiltrated every area of American life and were working to overthrow the American government. Virtually anyone with liberal or more extreme leftist views became suspect.

The senator and others in Congress held hearings to investigate the threat. Private organizations handed out lists of Americans they said were communist sympathizers. Many of the people on those lists lost their jobs. Much of the press was intimidated. Some individuals and publications were afraid to publish leftist opinions. Even much of the middle-of-the-road press, who felt that the "commie hunters" were violating other people's rights to free speech and political association, were afraid to criticize their methods. For the most part, however, the intimidation of the press was carried out without direct action by the government (other than the congressional hearings). The press was not so much censored as "chilled." It became timid, and out of fear it kept quiet.

During the American involvement in the Vietnam War, much of the press again engaged in voluntary censorship, as it had done during World War II. But this war was extremely controversial, and eventually conflict between the government and at least some elements of the press flared up. The most notable example of this was the so-called Pentagon Papers case. An ex-government employee named Daniel Ellsberg, who was opposed to America's role in the war, released a large number of secret government documents to the press. They revealed a wide range of covert (secret) American actions relating to the war.

The government went to the courts to get an order forbidding the press to publish the documents. That kind of censorship, in which something is censored that has not yet been published, is known as "prior restraint." A lower court granted the government a prior restraint order, but when the case was taken to the Supreme Court, the order was overturned. Prior restraint, the Court ruled, carried with it "a heavy burden of presumption against its constitutionality." The practice was not ruled out entirely, but it was made much more difficult for the government in the future.

RIGHTS IN CONFLICT

These, then, are two of America's most cherished rights: the right to a free press and the right to a fair trial.

When fundamental rights come into conflict with each other, as they sometimes do, it is up to the courts to decide between them. Which is the most important? Which must bend to accommodate the other in a particular case?

As we have seen, when the right to a free press has come into conflict with another right, such as the right of the government to be free from sedition, American courts have tended to side with freedom of the press. This has been particularly true in major cases, cases that set precedents for the future. It was true in the case of John Peter Zenger, before the American colonies ever became independent, and it was true in the Pentagon Papers case almost two and a half centuries later. These and many others are signs of the enormous value the courts place on the traditional American guarantee of freedom of the press.

The courts have a special kind of problem, however, when freedom of the press seems to come into conflict with the right to a fair trial. In such cases, they are asked to weigh the value of a free press against a right in which they have a particular interest, a right that involves the procedures and practices of the courts themselves.

Such conflicts, between press rights and trial rights, have tended over the years to center on questions of prejudicial publicity. How free can the press be in reporting on criminal cases in ways that might prejudice the community at large—and particularly the jury—against a defendant? Under the American system of justice, defendants are assumed to be innocent until and unless they are proven to be guilty. And yet the press has often stirred up communities (and even on some occasions, as we shall see, the whole country) against a defendant before he or she has even come to trial.

A whole new range of such conflicts opened up in the second decade of the twentieth century. It resulted from the development of the modern technologies of photography and broadcasting. These technologies allowed the press to cover trials in new ways, ways that many judges and other thoughtful observers saw as interfering fundamentally with the precious right to a fair trial. In the years since, controversy has raged—not just between the press and the judicial system, but within each of those institutions—over the use of those technologies in the nation's courtrooms.

How free should the press be to photograph and broadcast trial proceedings? To what extent, if any, should trial procedures be modified to accommodate the needs of the new technologies? Should cameras and microphones be allowed in the courtroom at all? These questions have become increasingly controversial in recent years as certain sensational cases have been literally televised across the nation. They are questions that have yet to be finally answered.

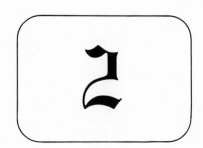

Surprise Witnesses: Cameras and Microphones in America's Courts

RADIO

Up until the mid-1920s, what was called "the press" was just that. It was a single medium, defined essentially by what could be printed by a printing press. It consisted of such subdivisions as newspapers, magazines and pamphlets, all of which had to be manufactured and transmitted more or less by hand.

But then, quite suddenly in the 1920s, the news *medium* of the press turned into the news *media*. It was then that radio was first used for news broadcasting. Radio technology, which had originally been developed for use in ship-to-shore and ship-to-ship communications where telegraphic wires could not be used, was destined to revolutionize mass communications—both news and entertainment—around the world.

At first, however, it was far from a mass medium. It began as the province of a small number of hobbyists, who built their own sets and spent their spare time trying to pull faint, scratchy signals out of the evening air. Then, in 1925, two commercial radio stations (WWJ in

Detroit and KDKA in Pittsburgh) went on the air, each claiming to be the first. Around that same time, mass-produced, cheap radio receiving sets became available to the general public, and a new age of electronic mass communication was underway.

By the mid-1920s, radio was recognized as the hottest entertainment medium in the country. Sales of phonograph records were in decline, and fewer and fewer people were going out to the movies. People were staying at home and listening to their radios. They were being regaled by a surprisingly varied menu of radio entertainment, ranging from dance music broadcast live from famous New York and Chicago nightclubs to special versions of stage hits performed by Broadway stars.

But people weren't looking to their radios just for entertainment. The value of radio as a medium for information was becoming clear. Radio provided the public with a new kind of window (or listening post) on the world. It was much more immediate, and therefore more exciting, than the newspapers that had previously formed the staple of news dissemination had ever been. All newspapers could do was to *tell* people about events *after* they had taken place. Radio could not only report on an event while it was going on, it could actually take its listeners there. It could let them hear great events for themselves, and do it live. This was something that no medium had ever been able to do before.

This ability of radio to take its listeners to events, to let people all across the country share in events at which they could not be physically present, was dramatically demonstrated early in 1925 when President Calvin Coolidge's inaugural address was broadcast over a nationwide network of radio stations. In a real—and completely new—sense, the citizens of the entire country were able to share, simultaneously, a great political and ceremonial event. It was the first time in history that such a thing had ever happened, and it underscored the power and significance of the new medium—a medium that had been considered little more than an eccentric toy just a few years before.

AGING GIANTS

It was inevitable that radio's unique (at that time) ability to bring distant events to its listeners would be used to cover a major trial.

Then, as now, many criminal trials were events of great public interest. Crime has always been a subject of major concern, and a trial, with the fate of a human being hanging in the balance, has a fascination all its own. The more violent and lurid the crime, and the more severe the possible penalty, the greater the fascination.

In a number of ways, a trial was an ideal kind of event for radio to cover. It is, after all, primarily a verbal affair. It can usually be listened to, and understood, without any kind of visual aid or extraneous explanation of what is taking place.

Radio is a vehicle for both entertainment and information, and a trial combines elements of both. A criminal trial is, of course, first and foremost a real event, and a very serious one. It deals with a real crime, or at least the accusation of a real crime, and the freedom—if not the life—of a real human being is at stake. But at the same time a trial has something of the artificial form of a classical drama.

An argument is presented—that a certain crime has been committed and that a particular person is guilty of it. That argument is challenged. What follows is a kind of staged battle between the forces of the defense and the prosecution, with the antagonism between them providing the necessary dramatic conflict. The trial unfolds in a series of confrontations. These take place both between the opposing attorneys and between each of them and the various witnesses. Like so many scenes in a play, these confrontations build to a climax. That climax is the verdict. Again as in a play, that climax resolves the conflict and reveals what is held to be the truth.

It is not surprising, then, that as early as the summer of 1925 the new medium was used to broadcast the proceedings of a major trial to listeners across the nation. What is surprising, however, is that this first trial to be broadcast involved an alleged crime that was neither violent nor lurid. What's more, the most severe penalty faced by the defendant if he was found guilty was a relatively small fine of $500. But, despite the apparently trivial nature of the alleged offense, the trial would prove to be one of the most sensational of the twentieth century.

The defendant in the case was a young biology teacher named John T. Scopes. The crime he was accused of was teaching the Darwinian theory of evolution to students in a public school in the small town of Dayton, Tennessee. Teaching Darwin's theory had been made a crime by Tennessee's Butler Act in March of 1925. The act read in part, "it should be unlawful for any teacher in any of the universities, normals and other public schools of the state . . . to teach any theory that denies the story of divine creation of man as taught in the Bible, and to teach instead that man is descended from a lower order of animals."

Scopes had broken the new law deliberately. Backed by the American Civil Liberties Union, which was providing his defense, he wanted to test the constitutionality of the law. The constitutional issue gave the case an importance that reached far beyond the boundaries of Dayton (pop. 1,800), but it was not enough to prompt the kind of international attention the Scopes trial ultimately received. That attention came from the presence at the trial, arguing opposite sides of the case, of two famous men: William Jennings Bryan and Clarence Darrow.

Bryan, then in his sixties, had been nominated three times for the office of president of the United States by the Democratic Party. He was a fiery speaker, and his so-called Cross of Gold speech had electrified the Democratic National Convention in Chicago in 1896 and won him the first of the three nominations. Throughout his long career, he had championed the cause of the "little man," particularly the farmers and the residents of rural and small-town America. His efforts on their behalf had made him a hero throughout the South and the Midwest. Although he had never actually been elected president, probably no other politician of his time was more revered by rural Americans.

Politically, he was a progressive and even a civil liberties advocate. But, like most of his supporters, Bryan was also a fundamentalist Christian. For him, as for them, the trial in Dayton would represent a battle between the revealed truth of the Bible and the blind error of atheistic science. "We cannot afford," he declared, "to have a system of education that destroys the religious faith of our children." In order to prevent such a thing, he announced that he would go to Dayton himself and help to prosecute John Scopes. From the moment of Bryan's announcement, it was sure that the attention of rural America would be focused on the courtroom in Dayton.

When he heard that Bryan was going to Tennessee, Clarence Darrow decided that he would go there, too. A famous defense lawyer from Chicago, Darrow resolved to counteract Bryan's support for the prosecution by helping out with Scopes's defense.

A few years older than Bryan, Darrow, too, had spent a long career championing the "little man." It was not always the same "little man," however. While Bryan worked largely on behalf of the farmers and residents of America's small towns, Darrow championed the nation's poorer city dwellers, many of whom were immigrants. Darrow had made much of his legal reputation defending union organizers accused of crimes against employers, and socialists and anarchists accused of crimes against the established social order. Where Bryan championed the cause of the small farmers against the banks that threatened to foreclose their mortgages, Darrow championed the factory workers against the factory owners who hired private armies to keep the workers from forming unions.

The two great champions of the "little man" had sometimes been allies. Darrow had even worked in two of Bryan's presidential campaigns. But they would not be allies in Dayton. Darrow was a strong supporter of free speech and free inquiry, rights he believed to be threatened by the Butler Act, and he was determined to fight both the act and his one-time friend in order to defend those rights. To Bryan's supporters—rural people with a deep distrust of the cities and of the people, often foreign immigrants, who lived in them—the Chicago lawyer was a dark figure, an arch villain. He was a city slicker, a defender of foreign troublemakers. What was worse, he was a declared agnostic. Many suspected him of actually being an atheist. To many rural Americans, the white-haired old man with the big belly and the wide suspenders looked very much like the devil himself. To many urban Americans, he was a hero.

The presence of the two aging giants—each revered by some and despised by others—captured national attention for the trial in Dayton. Thousands of people actually made the trip to the little town themselves, to be in on the excitement. Among them were hordes of revivalists, who set up tents in and around the town and gave fiery sermons condemning what they pronounced as "*evil*-ution," and all who would dare to teach such a thing to innocent schoolchildren. There were scores of hawkers as well, who peddled souvenirs of the case. Many of the souvenirs were shaped like monkeys since the popular understanding of the theory of evolution was that mankind was descended from the apes.

The most intrusive of the many visitors to Dayton that summer were the reporters. There were over a hundred of them. They came from all over the country, and from foreign nations as well. The best known among them was Baltimore's H. L. Mencken, who coined the phrase "Monkey Trial" to describe the case, a name by which it has been known ever since.

But, although they were not well-known personally, the most significant of the newspeople who descended on Dayton were not newspaper reporters and photographers, but the men from WGN, a Chicago radio station. They were the only ones, in those days before the sound movie camera, who could record the sounds of the trial and bring the famous voices of Bryan and Darrow to people all across the country. They were the ones who would make media and courtroom history by broadcasting the Monkey Trial into the homes of listeners across America.

THE MONKEY TRIAL

It might have been expected that the residents of the little town would resent this invasion by the big city newsmen, and that the trial judge would be appalled by it. The truth, however, was just the opposite. Most of Dayton's residents were delighted by the national attention the trial was getting. They looked to the masses of strangers as a financial windfall, and to the publicity as a possible long-term booster of tourism to a part of Tennessee that could badly use a new source of income. In fact, the loudest local complaint heard about the invasion of the city slickers was that it wasn't big enough.

As for Judge John T. Raulston of the Circuit Court of Rhea County, who tried the case, he seemed to be thrilled by the press's attention to him personally. Other judges in other courts might have found the media invasion of their courtroom—the stringing of cables, the whirring of the noisy movie cameras of the day (which could not record sound but made lots of it), the rude jockeying for position among the members of the press—

unacceptably disruptive. But not Judge Raulston. He seemed to glory in it. Far from trying to minimize the media's intrusion on the trial, he would even stop the proceedings to pose for the photographers. The atmosphere within the courtroom, then, was not very different from the circus atmosphere outside, and the media played a major part in establishing it.

The great media innovation of the trial—the radio coverage—was slow in getting started. Technical problems plagued the men from WGN, and as a result the early stages of the trial could not be broadcast.

Perhaps it was just as well. Very little seemed to happen. There was no question that John Scopes had taught the theory of evolution to his students. It was up to the defense to show, in essence, that the law and not the lawbreaker was in the wrong. This the defense tried to do by calling a number of distinguished expert witnesses. Those witnesses were to argue that the theory of evolution was not *necessarily* in conflict with the Bible (since the Bible could be, and was, interpreted in many ways). But Judge Raulston consistently denied the experts the right to testify, effectively gutting the defense's case. While there was some drama in all the legal maneuvering, it was not the kind of drama that would grip a nationwide radio audience. There was very little of the kind of fireworks that might have been expected from the titans, Bryan and Darrow.

Finally, in desperation, the defense took an unexpected step. It called William Jennings Bryan—who was a member of the prosecution team—as a witness for the *defense*. It wanted him to testify as an expert witness on the Bible. There was no legal obligation for Bryan to testify, but, prompted either by conviction, the challenge, or his ego, he agreed to take the stand. He would be examined by none other than Clarence Darrow.

Finally the battle would be joined. And at last, just in time, the radio crew was ready. They strung their cables and set up their three large microphones.

History was about to be made, and the radio broadcast was very much a part of that history. Even Judge Raulston was aware of the significance of radio's presence in his courtroom, although he had a rather egotistical view of it. "My gavel," he declared grandly, "will be heard around the world."

What followed—Darrow's examination of Bryan's fundamentalist beliefs—was one of the most memorable confrontations in American legal history. Quickly establishing that Bryan believed that everything written in the Bible was literally true, Darrow questioned him relentlessly, pointing out what he considered the scientific impossibility of some of the events recorded in the Bible. Bryan countered scientific argument with his own faith in the biblical accounts, an absolute faith shared by his many supporters. He refused to acknowledge that any of the Bible stories should be taken as allegories (symbolic stories expressing general truths), insisting that they were all true exactly as written.

Darrow heaped scorn, not on the Bible as such but on Bryan's interpretation of it. Did Bryan really believe that Jonah could survive in the belly of a great fish? Did Bryan really believe that the earth suddenly stood still in the heavens? Did Bryan have any idea what would happen if that actually took place?

Usually the verdict is the climax of a trial. In this case it was an anticlimax. Scopes was found guilty as charged (which he clearly was) and fined $100. The verdict was appealed, but the case was eventually dismissed on a technicality. The great constitutional issue was never settled. The trial discouraged other states from passing similar statutes, but the Butler Act remained in force in Tennessee until 1967, although it was rarely, if ever, enforced.

All that hardly seemed to matter to most people. What had fascinated listeners all over the country about the Monkey Trial was the confrontation between Bryan and Darrow. It was a rare moment in history, a battle between two giants defending two great beliefs, each shared passionately by a large group of Americans. Which of them won that battle depended to a great extent on the beliefs of those who listened to it. Bryan's fundamentalist supporters felt that he had won, while most other observers felt that Darrow had clearly embarrassed him.

Regardless of the outcome, radio had added a new and special dimension to the trial. It had allowed people all over the country to share in what was essentially a great national debate.

For the first time in history, Americans had been able to sit in their own homes and listen to the arguments in a trial, judging for themselves which were right and which were wrong. It was fortunate that in this first instance of electronic coverage of a trial the issue at stake was much larger than the guilt or innocence of a single individual. Over the next several years, the trials that would catch the attention of the new medium (as well as of the older media) would rarely be those that involved great national issues. Rather, they would be the most luridly sensational trials of the age. The press—and particularly the new electronic medium of radio—would cover them as much (if not more) for their entertainment value as for any public purpose.

THE *HAUPTMANN* CASE

The most luridly sensational trial of the next decade— and the one that attracted the most press attention—was that of Bruno Richard Hauptmann in 1935. He was accused of the kidnapping and murder of Charles A. Lindbergh III, the infant son of the aviator Charles Lindbergh.

The Hauptmann case was tailor-made for sensationalism. Lindbergh was an international hero. His solo flight across the Atlantic Ocean in the single-engined *Spirit of St. Louis* had electrified the world in 1927.

When he landed in France he was hailed as a hero there, and upon his return to the United States he was given the greatest welcome the country had ever seen. Everybody loved the man they called "Lucky Lindy." There was even a popular dance named after him. He was easily the most idolized man in America.

When Baby Lindbergh (as the press called the child) was stolen from his crib in the Lindbergh home at Hope-well, New Jersey, on May 1, 1932, the sympathy of the nation reached out to the still young hero and his wife, Anne. When a ransom was paid but the boy was not returned to his parents, that sympathy grew, and when the infant's dead body was found, it reached a depth and poignancy unprecedented in American history.

Then, more than two years later, when Hauptmann was found with a large part of the ransom money in his possession and arrested for the crimes, that sympathy turned into an equally unprecedented anger at the accused man.

If Lindbergh was the ideal hero for his place and time, Hauptmann was close to being the ideal villain. An immigrant from Germany who spoke English with a heavy accent, he seemed calculated to arouse the preju-dices of a large segment of the American population. The United States had fought a terrible war with Germany less than twenty years before, a war in which ten million people had been killed, and which was widely blamed on Germany. Many Americans still believed the outpouring of wartime propaganda, which had depicted the Ger-mans as vicious baby killers. Adolph Hitler had already come to power in Germany, and while the extent of the evil his government would do was not yet known, many Americans found the strutting little "führer" both repul-sive and typically German. They reacted to Bruno Rich-ard Hauptmann in much the same way. Some even thought that he looked like Hitler. What's more, it was discovered that in his native Germany, in the aftermath of the World War, with the economy of Germany in ruins, Hauptmann had become a burglar. He had a criminal record. If Lucky Lindy was a man people loved, Hauptmann was a man they loved to hate.

This was not true of all Americans, of course. There were many first or second generation Americans of German and other European descent who felt the prejudice inherent in the hostility to Hauptmann, and who wondered if he was being treated unfairly. Hauptmann maintained his innocence, and that added a certain element of suspense about the outcome of the case that helped to inflame the interest of both the public and the press.

CIRCUS IN FLEMINGTON

The press—newspaper, magazine, radio, and newsreel (now sound newsreel)—rushed en masse to Flemington, New Jersey, where the trial was to be held. Once there, they swarmed around any trial participants they could find like so many sharks in a feeding frenzy. Their antics, both within the Hunterdon County Courthouse and without, would alarm many serious observers, upset the trial judge, and ultimately result in one of the most significant restrictions on the freedom of the press in American history.

They came in large numbers, more than four times more of them than had descended on Dayton a decade before. Among them were some of the leading names in American journalism and literature. The Pulitzer prize–winning novelist Edna Ferber was there to cover the trial, as was the famous short story writer Damon Runyon. Other popular journalists such as Walter Winchell (who would later serve as the voice of *The Untouchables* on television), Alexander Woollcott and Adela Rogers St. John were there, too, along with scores and scores of others. Many of them were cameramen of one kind or another. The major newspapers and magazines had sent their crack photographers, and the newsreel companies had sent some of their top cinematographers.

(It would turn out to be the newsreelmen who would cause the most trouble of all.) Between them the reporters, cameramen, and broadcasters managed to manufacture a circus atmosphere in Flemington, New Jersey in 1935 that was not very different from that in Dayton, Tennessee in 1925.

In Dayton, however, nobody had cared. The judge (who was shortly to run for reelection) had positively welcomed the publicity, and both the prosecution and the defense were pleased to get their arguments across to as much of the American public as possible. The actual verdict of the trial was relatively unimportant to all the participants (and was, in any case, a foregone conclusion).

In Flemington, however, there was a very real question of guilt or innocence involved (although to see and hear many of the press reports, which clearly implied Hautpmann was guilty, one wouldn't have thought so). A man's life was at stake. So was his constitutional right to a fair trial. And the judge in the case, Judge Thomas W. Trenchard, was very much concerned with protecting that right. He attempted, insofar as he could, to set rules of conduct and procedure for the press that would assure a proper judicial atmosphere in his courtroom. (The press, as we will see, did everything they could to get around those rules.) But he could do nothing about the press's conduct outside the courtroom. They flocked around the participants in the trial as they came to and from the court. Flashbulbs popped, cameras whirred, questions were shouted, microphones were shoved rudely in front of lawyers' and witnesses' faces.

The jury was sequestered. That is, for the duration of the trial they were lodged in a hotel across the street from the courthouse. The object of this was to keep them from being influenced by any of the massive publicity that surrounded the case, and to keep them from discussing the case with anyone.

Unfortunately, however, a large proportion of the

huge press corps covering the trial was staying at the same hotel. They ate in the same dining room as the jury, and there is little doubt that at least some members of the jury heard them discussing the case amongst themselves. Since most of the press, like most of the public, was convinced that Hauptmann was guilty, the possible prejudicial effect of all this was obvious.

If the press's activities outside the courtroom were rowdy and irresponsible, their activities inside the courtroom were not much better. Those activities came to an almost comic climax with the announcement of the verdict. The judge, doing his best to keep order in his court to the last, had ordered that the courtroom be locked during the announcement of the verdict. It was a solemn moment, and he did not want an unseemly (and possibly even dangerous) rush to the doors by the journalists, each trying to be the first to get the story out to an eagerly awaiting public.

Many of the newsmen present had made elaborate arrangements to try to get around the judge's order. The Associated Press reporter went so far as to sneak a shortwave radio transmitter into the courtroom concealed in a briefcase. He planned to use it to transmit a coded signal to a confederate waiting outside the courtroom, thus revealing the jury's verdict as soon as it was given.

Unknown to the AP reporter, however, another journalist had had the same idea, and was waiting poised with his own shortwave transmitter and his own even more elaborate code. When the jury entered the courtroom, this reporter transmitted his own prearranged code announcing that fact. His signal was picked up not only by his own accomplice, but by the AP man outside the court as well. It happened that that signal, announcing the jury's arrival, was the same as the AP's signal for the verdict "guilty, with life imprisonment." The AP immediately sent out the word of the supposed verdict to its twelve hundred subscribing newspapers, as well as to a major radio service that it also supplied.

When the jury announced its real verdict a short time later, the AP realized that it had made a mistake. The real verdict was guilty, all right, but the jury had called for the death penalty. The mighty Associated Press had outsmarted itself and misinformed its public.

The actual announcement of the verdict, meanwhile, set off a number of other schemes among the newspeople present to get the story out of the locked courtroom. One of the reporters had to be restrained from throwing a color-coded iron ball out through a closed courtroom window.

The winner in the contest to scoop the story was Francis Toughill of the Philadelphia *Record*, who had managed to smuggle a telephone headset into the court-room. He had cut into the court's own telephone line, and, hiding in a balcony out of sight of the judge, he simply telephoned the *Record* as soon as the jury foreman delivered the verdict.

BETRAYAL

But the most blatant of all the violations of the judge's orders—and the one that would do the most to prompt the coming restrictions on the press—had taken place long before the verdict. It had been committed not by the overzealous newspapermen but by the makers of the newsreels.

Newsreels were extremely popular in 1935. They were the closest thing then available to today's television news broadcasts. They provided the movie audiences of the day with motion picture and sound views of major news events—ranging from the sights and sounds of foreign wars to Atlantic City beauty contests. Audiences thrilled to the sense that the newsreels gave them of witnessing history as it was taking place. So much so, in fact, that newsreels formed a regular part of the bill in virtually every movie theater in the country. They were usually shown between the two feature movies that constituted the main attractions on the bill, and they were updated each week. In the larger cities there were even some theaters that devoted themselves entirely to the showing of newsreels. These were often every bit as popular as the theaters that relied on the standard Hollywood fare.

Much like television news reports today, newsreel features tended to be brief and superficial. Unlike television news, however, they were unashamedly entertainment oriented. Although they often covered events that were serious in nature, they seldom made any pretense of covering them in a serious way. They were usually narrated in booming tones calculated to add excitement to what was being shown. Virtually always male, the newsreel narrators sounded less like a modern television newscaster than like a TV game show announcer informing the contestants of all the wonderful prizes they stand to win.

Still, the newsreel was a major medium of information for the moviegoing public of the day, and the medium had a valid claim to all the rights and privileges granted to the rest of the press. Judge Raulston had eagerly allowed them to be present in his courtroom during the Scopes trial (although in those days, they were not equipped for sound). Judge Trenchard, much less enthusiastically, allowed them to be present in his courtroom as well.

He did, however, place conditions on the filming of newsreels in the courtroom. In order to protect the rights of everyone involved, and to assure decorum in the court, he asked that no filming be done while he was on the bench. That meant that there must be no filming of the trial proceedings themselves. The courtroom could be filmed, and the defendant, witnesses, jury, and others as they entered and left the courtroom, or if and when they milled around the room when the court was not in session. But between the gavels that opened and closed sessions of the court, the camera had to be turned off.

This restriction also applied to the scores of still photographers, who were also forbidden to shoot while the trial was in progress.

All six newsreel companies—Paramount, Metrotone, Hearst, Fox, Pathé, and Universal—seemed to accept the limitation. Emphasizing their cooperation, they agreed to share a single camera, supplying operators for it on a revolving basis, with each company getting a separate print of all the film shot. They even went so far as to enclose the camera in a soundproof hood, which would absolutely minimize any disruption it might cause in the court. Everything seemed perfectly in order as the trial began, and for most of the trial's duration the judge continued to believe that it was.

In reality, however, the newsreel makers had no intention of abiding by the judge's restrictions. For them, the soundproof hood over the camera had a special function—it disguised the fact that they were violating the judge's conditions by running the camera when the court was in session. In this underhanded way, they captured most of the important moments of the trial, including the testimony of the defendant Hauptmann himself, which was the trial's dramatic high point.

At first, the companies didn't intend to show their films until after the trial was over. But near the end of the trial they heard rumors that a new film company, The March of Time, was prepared to film and release a reenactment of the major events of the trial. In order to undercut the competition, the newsreel companies went ahead and released their films of the trial itself. All across the country people flocked to the theaters to see them. Back in Flemington, Judge Trenchard was incensed. He ordered the newsreel camera barred from his courtroom, and for good measure he threw out the still cameras as well. The newspapers were shocked, since they hadn't violated the agreement. (Two of them had published stills from the newsreels after they'd already been shown in the theaters, but that was all.) Still, the judge remained firm. There were to be no more pictures taken in his court.

Since at least one photograph of the reading of the verdict has survived, it's clear that even this direct order of the judge was violated. But the important fact remained this: cameras had been banned from a courtroom. It was a specific order that would soon be turned into a general rule.

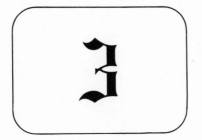

Thrown out of Court: Cameras and Microphones Are Banned

CANON 35

The behavior of the press at the Hauptmann trial was not unique. The 1920s and '30s were decades of fierce competition between newspapers and other news organizations. Radio and newsreels were trying desperately to build audiences. Each major city had several large newspapers, each trying to grab as many readers as possible from the others. Consequently, each reporter fought with all the others to be first with a story, or to find some new sensational gimmick to thrill his or her audience.

But the Hauptmann trial was by far the most heavily publicized trial of its time. As a result, it drew more attention than any other to the irresponsible excesses of the press. Those excesses seriously troubled many observers, on several grounds.

The most important ground had to do with the right of a defendant to a fair trial. While most observers who have studied the trial believe that Hauptmann probably was, in fact, guilty as charged, many doubt that the trial was truly fair. At least partly, they blame this on the activities of the press, which strongly prejudiced the public against him and may have influenced the jury. Even several of those who believe that Hauptmann almost certainly would have been found guilty in any case believe that without the excessive clamor from the press he would have only been sentenced to life imprisonment rather than to death.

Aside from the question of the fairness of the trial, many judges deplored the effect of press excesses on the decorum of the court. A courtroom, they believed, must be a dignified and even solemn place, where the truth can be sought in a calm and reasoned way. Such press behavior destroyed the judicial atmosphere necessary for such a search.

There was another aspect to what had taken place at Flemington that bothered some serious observers even more. They felt that the kind of press coverage that reached its peak in the Hauptmann trial distorted not only the trial process, but the whole system of values on which the search for justice is based. Even the journalistic magazine *Editor and Publisher*, which had a basic sympathy with the journalists, was troubled by this. "If the life of one man and the unhappiness of hundreds are to be commercialized for the benefit of entertainment, of radio broadcasters, newspaper publishers, newsreel producers," it argued, ". . . then the ancient institution of trial by a jury of peers is without meaning."

The legal profession debated the question of what to do about such excesses for two years. Then, in 1937, they came up with a partial solution. In that year, the House of Delegates of the American Bar Association adopted Judicial Canon 35. It declared not only that all cameras should be banned from the nation's courts, but that all broadcasting of trials by radio should also be forbidden. Such activities, it maintained, "detract from the essential dignity of the proceedings, distract participants and witnesses in giving testimony, and create misconceptions with respect thereto in the mind of the public and should not be permitted."

Canon 35 did not carry with it the force of law. It was really little more than a recommendation on the part of the nation's most influential legal association. But in the decades that followed it would be, in the words of Herbert Brucker, writing in the *Saturday Review*, "revered by many a judge and lawyer as though it had come down from Sinai with the rest of the Commandments."

Although not followed in every state, it largely accomplished its purpose. From 1935 on, all photographing and all broadcasting of trials were effectively banned from most of the nation's state courtrooms.

An even more effective ban was put on the broadcasting of trials held in the federal courts. Acting from much the same motives as the American Bar Association, the Congress of the United States passed Rule 53 of the Federal Rules of Criminal Procedure. This rule, which has the force of law, absolutely prohibits the broadcasting of trials or other business conducted in any federal court anywhere in the United States.

TEXAS v. ESTES

Billie Sol Estes was one of the most fascinating characters in the huge state of Texas. A poor boy from the farm country of West Texas, he made himself rich in the fertilizer and grain storage businesses. By 1962, when he was thirty-seven years old, he already owned all or part of forty-one different companies, including a newspaper in the little town of Pecos, Texas, where he lived and from which he ran his economic empire. His wealth was estimated at somewhere around $50 million.

But it wasn't just the fact that he was rich that made Billie Sol Estes fascinating to those who knew him. It was the mass of seeming contradictions that made up his complex character. A devout Christian, he seemed to take equal pleasure in driving rival businessmen to bankruptcy and in giving large sums of money to charity. A wealthy man in a conservative state, he was a liberal Democrat. He gave substantial donations to the Texas Democratic Party. Some of its more liberal leaders even considered running him for governor in the 1960 election.

Billie Sol was, in Texas parlance, a "wheeler-dealer." He was clearly a young man on the move, and the direction he was moving in was up. Until March 1962. It was then, at a time when he seemed to have everything a young man could want, that the FBI arrested him. Within the next few months he was charged with a number of crimes, ranging from simple fraud to corrupting officials of the Department of Agriculture and illegally conspiring to corner the chemical fertilizer market.

Estes' wealth and his ties to the Texas Democratic Party made his case the object of national attention. An extra element of sensationalism was added to the case when a Department of Agriculture official who had questioned Estes was shot to death. The murderer, or murderers, were unknown.

Estes was charged with some state crimes and some federal. The first to come to trial was a state swindling charge. It was originally scheduled to be tried in Estes' home town, but the extreme publicity prompted a move to Tyler, Texas, more than five hundred miles away. The change did nothing to deter the national press, which flocked to Tyler as they had flocked to Dayton and Flemington years before.

The publicity was intense. The newspaper coverage of the case alone filled eleven volumes even before the trial began. When a pretrial hearing was scheduled at Tyler, the courtroom was, predictably, jammed. Most of the observers were members of the press. Once again, representatives of all the major big city papers, the national wire services and the radio networks were gathered together in a single courtroom. This time, however, they were joined by a new kind of press contingent, the television crews.

Canon 35, which had been aimed at still cameras and radio broadcasting when it was first passed in 1937, had since been amended to include a ban on television broadcasting. But Canon 35, as already stated, was not a law. The actual laws under which a state court must function are laid down by the legislatures of the individual states. Most states had gone along with the principles of Canon 35, but Texas was one of only two that had not. (The other was Colorado, which became the first state to allow television into its courtrooms in 1956). In Texas, the decision of whether to allow the cameras was left up to the trial judge of each particular case.

The defense moved that television be banned from the pretrial hearing for the *Estes* case. The affair was already notorious enough, and the presence of television would only magnify its sensational aspects. Besides, the cameras would disrupt the proceedings. The judge, however, ruled that the cameras could stay. The press had a right to cover the hearing, and the public had a right to know what went on there. The judge's decision would have far-reaching consequences. It would make the *Estes* case the basis for the first Supreme Court ruling on the legality of allowing criminal trials to be televised.

The decision's immediate consequence, however, was to turn the Tyler courtroom into a kind of bedlam. There were at least twelve cameramen (still, motion picture, and television) jockeying for position among the crowd of other journalists and ordinary spectators. As Justice Clark of the Supreme Court would later describe the scene: "Cables and wires were snaked across the courtroom floor, three microphones were on the judge's bench and others were beamed at the jury box and the council table . . . the activities of the television crews and news photographers led to considerable disruption of the hearings." Another chronicler would note that the cameramen behaved so badly, it was as if their main purpose was to convince the judiciary never to allow them into a courtroom again.

When the case finally came to trial, the judge took steps to keep the cameramen under control. A special booth was provided for them—at the broadcasters' expense—in the back of the courtroom. An opening in the front of the booth allowed them to photograph and record the proceedings.

The defense was still not happy with the cameras being there and repeatedly objected. Some of these objections were upheld by the trial judge, and consequently only certain portions of the trial were actually televised. Other than the state's opening and closing arguments (and due to a technical malfunction, even the opening argument was recorded without pictures), only the delivery and receipt of the verdict were actually carried live on television.

The judge permitted the rest of the trial to be videotaped, but without sound. Using their own judgment, the television people actually only bothered to tape portions of it. Brief segments of the tapes were then used by various television stations and networks during their regular news broadcasts. They were used chiefly, in the words of Justice Clark, "as a backdrop" to reporters' summations of the trial proceedings.

Billie Sol Estes was found guilty as charged. He appealed the conviction all the way up to the Supreme Court. That appeal would result in the first Supreme Court decision on the constitutionality of the photographing and broadcasting of criminal trials.

ESTES v. TEXAS

Estes claimed in his appeal that his constitutonal right to a fair trial had been violated by the television coverage. Both the pretrial hearing and portions of the trial itself had been televised, despite his objections. His attorneys argued that this constituted a denial of the due process guaranteed by the Fifth and Fourteenth Amendments to the Constitution of the United States. The presence of the television cameras had added to the notoriety of the case and aroused prejudice against Estes. What's more, the cameras themselves had been a distraction in the courtroom, interfering with the proper functioning of the trial.

The State of Texas responded that Estes had failed to demonstrate any actual prejudice traceable to the presence of television. The so-called distractions caused by the cameras were "psychological considerations" which were "purely hypothetical." Most importantly of all, argued the state, the Sixth Amendment guarantees a "public trial." The public has a right to know what goes on in their courts, and television is a legitimate way for them to exercise that right to know. The court, therefore, does not have the power to "suppress, edit, or censor events which transpire in proceedings before it." Furthermore, televising trials helps to enlighten the general public about the trial process and would result in a deeper public respect for the courts.

The Texas Court of Criminal Appeals denied Estes' claim that television had deprived him of due process. The Supreme Court of the United States, however, by the close vote of five to four, disagreed. They overturned Estes' conviction.

The majority opinion, which would stand as the opinion of the Court, was written by Justice Tom Clark. Because of its great importance as a legal precedent, we will review it here.

Clark began by briefly outlining the arguments in the case. He then described the "considerable disruption" caused by the cameramen at the pretrial hearing. The atmosphere, he commented, "was not one of that judicial serenity and calm to which [Estes] was entitled."

Dismissing arguments that the pretrial hearing should not be considered in the appeal, Clark maintained that publicity during pretrial "may be more harmful than publicity during the trial for it may well set the community opinion as to guilt or innocence." In the case of the *Estes* pretrial hearing specifically, he stated that all the publicity "could only have impressed those present, and also the community at large, with the notorious character of [Estes] as well as the proceeding." In other words, it helped create a climate in which the public, including potential jurors, could have been prejudiced against the defendant.

The majority opinion went on to emphasize the importance of a public trial to a free society. That importance was summed up by Justice Clark: "The purpose . . . of a public trial was to guarantee that the accused would be fairly dealt with and not unjustly condemned. History has proven that secret tribunals were instruments of oppression." That having been said, he went on to reject the argument that the First Amendment guarantee of freedom of the press extends "a right . . . to televise from the courtroom, and that to refuse to honor this privilege is to discriminate between the newspapers and television." Television and radio reporters had the same right of access to the courtroom as newspaper reporters had, he declared. It was the same right the general public had. But the right was limited for everyone. "The news reporter is not permitted to bring his typewriter or printing press," Clark explained, so why, he implied, should the television reporter be allowed to bring his camera? Interestingly, he did not rule out changes in a future in which media technology itself undergoes major changes. "When the advances in these arts permit reporting . . . by television without its present hazards to a fair trial," he wrote, "we will have another case."

Taking up Texas's claim that no prejudice had been actually proved in the case, Clark contended that "at times" a given procedure "involved such a probability that prejudice will result that it is deemed inherently lacking in due process." The televising of Estes' trial, both he and the Court believed, was just such a procedure.

As for the question of television's legitimacy as a means of ensuring the public's right to know: "[T]he chief function of our judicial machinery is to ascertain the truth. The use of television, however, cannot be said to contribute materially to this objective. Rather, its use amounts to an injection of an irrelevant factor into court proceedings. . . . In addition experience teaches that there are numerous situations in which it might cause actual unfairness—some so subtle as to defy detection. . . ." He then went on to point out some of those possibilities. Among them were television's possible effects on jurors. As soon as it is even announced that a trial will be televised, he said, "[t]he whole community, including prospective jurors, becomes interested in all the morbid details surrounding it." Once jurors are chosen, they might well be "distracted" by the presence of television. "We are all self-conscious and uneasy when being televised," he declared, and jurors' minds might well be "preoccupied with the telecasting rather than with the testimony." In many states (although not in Texas, where jurors were sequestered) jurors might see videotapes of portions of the trial in which they were serving. There was a real concern that they might be influenced by the portions of the trial the television stations found worthy of televising. What's more, any possible retrial might be jeopardized by the jury pool having watched all or part of the original trial on television. In short, the bad effects of televising trials on potential and actual jurors were many and complex.

Clark then went on to consider television's effect on witnesses. "The impact upon a witness of the knowledge that he is being viewed by a vast audience is simply incalculable," he asserted. Some might become frightened, he suggested, others cocky; others might overdramatize, and so on. All such effects would "impede the search for truth," which was at the heart of the trial process. Such effects would be impossible to prove, but "we all know from experience that they exist."

Having discussed the problems television might cause for the jurors and witnesses, Clark moved on to the problems it presents to the trial judge. "[The judge's] job is to make certain that the accused receives a fair trial. This most difficult task requires his undivided attention." The presence of television only complicates the trial process and makes the judge's job more difficult. It is particularly distracting in those states where judges are elected. Television then "becomes a political weapon, which . . . diverts his attention from the task at hand."

Worst of all, perhaps, was television's impact on the defendant. For him or her, as Clark saw it, television's "presence is a form of mental—if not physical—harassment, resembling a police line-up or the third degree." He went on to state, in one of the more memorable passages of his decision, that a defendant "is entitled to his day in court, not in a stadium." By its very presence, television excites the public, making it more likely that they'll believe the defendant to be guilty. "The heightened public clamor resulting from radio and television coverage will inevitably result in prejudice."

This, then, was the reasoning that led Clark, along with the majority of the Supreme Court, to conclude that Billie Sol Estes' right to due process had been violated by the televising of portions of his trial.

4

Back on Appeal

THE REAL MEANING
OF *ESTES*

The Supreme Court's decision in the *Estes* case seemed to be a devastating blow to television's future in the courtroom. Justice Clark had recited a long list of the dangers involved in bringing cameras into the courtroom, and had acknowledged no benefits whatsoever. "Trial by television," he had written, "is . . . foreign to our system."

It was true that four of the justices had voted against the decision. But even they were less than encouraging to television's proponents. The major dissenting opinion, written by Justice Potter Stewart, had itself declared: ". . . the introduction of television into a courtroom is, at least in the present state of the art, an extremely unwise policy." With the majority of the Court ruling that television was "foreign" to the trial process, and even a dissenter calling its presence in a court "extremely unwise," it is not surprising that many observers regarded the decision as all but fatal to any chance of televising trials in the United States. In fact, much of the news media itself reported the decision in that light.

Among other observers who felt that the Court had, in effect, banned television from the nation's courtrooms were many judges. Their attitude was demonstrated in a ruling made by a circuit court judge in Dane County, Wisconsin, who was called upon to decide whether a Madison, Wisconsin, public television station would be allowed to televise a civil trial involving actions of the Madison city government.

This case was about as far removed from the sensationalism and notoriety of the *Estes* case as a trial could be. After examining a plan submitted by the television station, Judge Edwin M. Wilkie found that the televising "would be accomplished without disrupting such judicial proceedings and without prejudicing the rights of the parties in that the equipment used, including cameras, microphones and other electronic equipment would be unobtrusively placed and would not . . . have a psychological effect upon participants in the trial." What's more, "it would not in any respect encroach upon full and fair trial of the case and would not result in the reproduction or telecast of court proceedings to the public in such way as to affect the result of the trial."

The case was to be heard before the judge himself, without a jury to be adversely affected by the presence of the cameras. Despite all this (and despite the fact that the judge admitted that if he were able to exercise his own discretion in the matter, he would allow the proceedings to be televised), he ruled that television cameras could *not* be allowed in the courtroom. For his reason, he cited *Estes*. That decision of the Supreme Court, he explained, "amounts to" a ruling that telecasting of a trial constitutes a "*per se*" denial of due process.

That was a common reading of the *Estes* decision, but not the only one. Some more perceptive observers recognized that *Estes* was neither so devastating nor so final as it seemed. One of the justices who had voted with the majority had done so on the specific circumstances of the case, and not on general constitutional grounds. His vote—necessary for the Court to have a majority—rested on his belief that prejudice had been sufficiently demonstrated in that particular case to justify overturning the Texas verdict.

The significance of this was explained in a dissenting opinion written by Justice William Brennan. "[O]nly four of the five justices voting to reverse rest on the proposition that televised criminal trials are constitutionally infirm, whatever the circumstances. . . . Thus today's decision is *not* a blanket constitutional prohibition against the televising of state trials."

Brennan recognized that the really important thing about the *Estes* decision was not what the Court had done, but what it had *not* done. It had not declared the broadcasting of trials unconstitutional.

Ironically, in the nearly three decades between the passage of Canon 35 and the *Estes* decision, only two states, Texas and Colorado, had gone against the American Bar Association's recommendations and allowed cameras into their courtrooms; but in the two decades following *Estes*, a great many new states began to experiment with television in their courts.

It didn't happen all at once. *Estes* had—perhaps unintentionally—opened the door, but few states were eager to rush through it. In time, however, a number of factors combined to encourage them.

The media, particularly the fast-growing television industry, lobbied for greater access to the courts. Their lobbying seemed to gain in effectiveness over time, greatly helped by technological advances that made television's presence less distracting in the courtroom.

New judges came onto the bench, and younger judges replaced older ones in positions of influence. Many of these newer and younger judges tended to be more comfortable with television, more familiar and experienced with it. They were often more open to the idea of allowing it into their courts than their older, more traditional predecessors.

While all this was taking place, there was a gradual change in the political climate of the country as well. In many ways the nation was becoming more conservative. A part of that new conservatism had to do with the rights of the states as opposed to the rights of the federal government. There was a widespread feeling that the federal government had gotten too powerful, and that the state governments were too weak. Along with this feeling came a greater assertiveness on the part of many state governments vis-à-vis the federal government.

The federal judiciary steadfastly refused to allow cameras and microphones into the federal courts. In doing so, they were buttressed not only by Rule 53 of the Federal Rules of Criminal Procedure, but also by the prestigious Judicial Conference of the United States. This conference, made up of twelve chief judges and twelve district judges, and chaired by Chief Justice Warren Burger of the United States Supreme Court, bitterly opposed any intrusion of cameras or broadcasting—and particularly of *television* broadcasting—into the federal courts. But as the sentiment for states' rights grew throughout the 1970s, federal opposition to television seemed less like a reason for the states to follow suit.

As a result of all these factors, there was a growing willingness on the part of the states to experiment with television. The experiments were tentative at first. They did not simply open up their courtrooms to the cameras. Instead, they set strict standards as to what could be televised and what could not. Many states, for example, refused to allow television if a defendant objected. All insisted that the placing of cameras and the activities allowed to the cameramen be kept under the strict control of the trial judge.

In 1978, a conference of chief justices from many states met to consider the issue. They decided that each state's policy on television should be left up to the highest court in that individual state. At the time of the conference, some seventeen states had ongoing experiments with television in their courts. In the wake of the conference's decision, fifteen more began to plan experiments of their own.

Despite all this activity, involving more than half the states, the legal fraternity as a whole remained dubious about the value of television. According to a survey of attorneys in 1979, 75 percent of them believed that television would be a distraction to witnesses. More than half believed that it would have an unfortunate effect on their colleagues as well. They felt that both lawyers and judges would "grandstand" to impress the viewing audience at home. What's more, only 37 percent felt that televising trials would improve the public's understanding and respect for the American judicial system.

Despite this less than heartfelt endorsement of television in the courtroom, the experiments continued.

THE FLORIDA EXPERIMENT

Among the key states experimenting with television was Florida. Its initial experiment was carried out over the course of a year, from July of 1977 to June of 1978. During that time, cameras were allowed into the state's criminal courts under strict regulations. Among them: there could be only one television camera, the jury was not to be photographed, and the camera could only be run during those portions of the trial specified by the judge.

An important feature of the Florida experiment was that it did not acknowledge any constitutional right for the television cameras to be in the court. They were to be allowed, but only on the sufferance of the judge, and under his or her control. The experiment was, however, very generous to the media in another way. It allowed them to broadcast the trials with or without the consent of the accused. This was significant because in the ten states that allowed cameras only with the consent of the accused, that consent was rarely given.

The Florida experiment was only one of several, but it was of special importance because it would ultimately prompt the most important United States Supreme

Court decision to date on the question of television in the courtroom.

CHANDLER v. FLORIDA

The televised trial that would result in that landmark decision was a seemingly insignificant criminal trial in Miami Beach, Florida. Two men, Noel Chandler and Robert Granger, were charged with burglarizing a restaurant. Their case came to trial in 1977, during the time the Florida courts were experimenting with television.

It was not a sensational case, like *Scopes, Hauptmann* and *Estes* had been. Its only even moderately sensational aspect was the fact that the defendants had been Miami Beach policemen. Consequently, the television coverage of the trial was not extensive. Altogether, less than three minutes of the trial were actually televised.

Still, when the two men were found guilty, they appealed on the grounds that their constitutional right to a fair trial had been violated by television. They argued that the presence of the television camera had polluted the judicial atmosphere. Their claim that the television coverage was biased against them was supported by the fact that the entire three-minute broadcast had been taken from the prosecution's side of the case. But their fundamental objection was not *what* had been broadcast but that any part of the trial had been broadcast at all. They based their claim on *Estes.* They argued that Justice Brennan had been wrong in his dissent, and that the majority of the justices who had voted to overturn *Estes* had been right. Televising a trial was inherently a denial of due process and therefore unconstitutional. The *Estes* decision should be interpreted as exactly what Brennan had said it was not—"a blanket constitutional prohibition against the televising of state trials."

The convicted men and their attorneys might well have expected a sympathetic hearing from the Supreme Court. True, the *Estes* decision had been close—five to four—but the Court was considerably more conservative in 1981, when it met to consider *Chandler,* than it had been in 1965. The more conservative the justices, the more reluctant they might be to break the tradition of barring cameras of all kinds from the courtroom. Not only that, the 1981 Court was headed by Chief Justice Warren Burger, who had a well-known distaste for television cameras both inside the court and out, and who was a strong supporter of the ban on cameras of all kinds from the federal courts.

It was something of a surprise, then, when the Supreme Court handed down its judgment. It denied the appeal. Even more surprisingly, the decision was a unanimous eight to zero (with one justice present but not voting). Remarkably, the majority opinion upholding Florida's right to allow cameras into its courts was written by none other than Chief Justice Warren Burger himself.

In his opinion Burger readily acknowledged some of the problems that extensive news coverage of trials could cause. "Over the past 50 years," he wrote, "some criminal cases characterized as 'sensational' have been subjected to extensive coverage by news media, sometimes seriously interfering with the conduct of the proceedings and creating a setting wholly inappropriate for the administration of justice." But the only question the Court had before it in the *Chandler* case was "the limited question of the Florida Supreme Court's authority to promulgate [its rule] for the trial of cases in Florida's courts."

As for the argument that the televising of trials is inherently a denial of due process and that *Estes* should be taken "as announcing a per se constitutional rule to that effect," Burger disagreed.

"We conclude that *Estes* is not to be read as a constitutional rule barring still photographic, radio and television coverage in all cases and in all circumstances," he declared. What's more, the Court was not about to make such a rule in the *Chandler* case. "An absolute constitutional ban on broadcast coverage of trials cannot be justified simply because there is a danger that, in some

[63]

cases, prejudicial broadcast accounts of pretrial and trial events may impair the ability of jurors to decide the issue of guilt or innocence uninfluenced by extraneous matter." In that limited respect, at least, the broadcast media were to be treated the same as the traditional media. "The risk of juror prejudice in some cases does not justify an absolute ban on news coverage of trials by the printed media; so also the risk of such prejudice does not warrant an absolute constitutional ban on all broadcast coverage."

Instead, "the appropriate safeguard against such prejudice is the defendant's right to demonstrate that the media's coverage of his case—be it printed or broadcast—compromised the ability of the particular jury that heard the case to adjudicate fairly." This the defendants in the *Chandler* case had failed to do.

In a partial explanation of why the *Chandler* decision was so different from that of the earlier Court in *Estes*, Burger pointed to the changes in television technology in the intervening years. "It is urged, and some empirical data are presented, that many of the negative factors found in *Estes*—cumbersome equipment, cables, distracting lighting, numerous camera technicians—are less substantial factors today than they were at that time." The disruption caused by the presence of the broadcasting media's technicians and equipment—which had troubled thoughtful jurists from the time of the *Scopes* trial on—was ceasing to be a major factor in the eyes of the Court.

Burger concluded that Florida should be allowed to "permit the electronic media to cover trials in its state courts." He acknowledged that "dangers lurk in this, as in most, experiments," but he went on to affirm that "the states must be free to experiment" anyway.

For the long, often uneasy relationship between the press and the courts, *Chandler* was a landmark decision. However unenthusiastically, the Supreme Court had finally ruled that the televising of criminal trials was *not* unconstitutional in the United States.

[64]

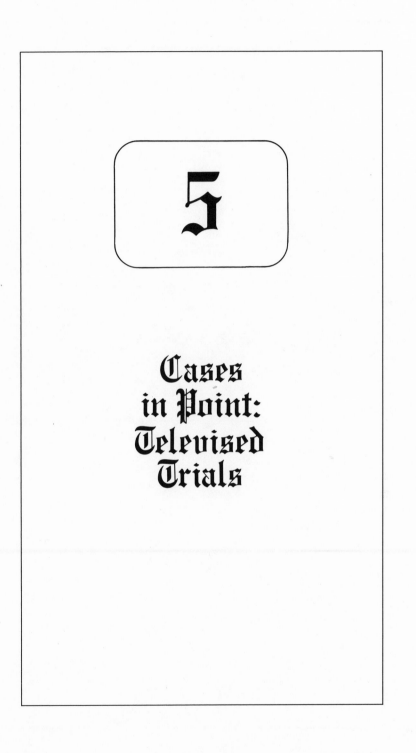

5

Cases in Point: Televised Trials

COMMON PRACTICE

In the years following the *Chandler* decision, many more states moved to open up their courtrooms to television. By the end of 1984, forty states had rules that allowed television to record at least some trials under some circumstances. The final decision in any particular case was usually left up to the trial judge.

For the most part, television's new presence in the courtrooms produced surprisingly little controversy. One reason for this was the fact that *Chandler* had made appeals based on that presence less likely to succeed. Another was the fact that judges continued to ban the cameras from the most sensational trials to come before them. When the wealthy heiress Patricia Hearst was tried for alleged terrorist activity, for example, television was kept out, as it was when Jean Harris was tried for the murder of her lover Dr. Tarnower in another highly publicized case. Such trials continued to be covered by television the way they had been covered for years before *Chandler*. Reporters would be televised standing outside the courtroom, or on the street outside the courthouse, giving brief verbal reports of the trial proceedings. When there was a great deal of interest in the participants, television would show sketches of them as they looked to an artist who had been present in the court.

Another reason for the lack of controversy over the cameras was the fact that the televising of trial proceedings tended to be local and severely limited in duration. Time on local television news shows is precious. They have a lot of news to cover in a short period of time. Most stations simply were not interested in using up a lot of that time in televising extended portions of trials. Trials can sometimes be as dramatic and exciting as anything to be found on entertainment television, but much of any trial process is routine, dull, and repetitive. In order for a station to capture the dramatic moments of a trial for its viewers, it might have to keep a camera and one or more technicians in the courtroom for days at a time, waiting for the fireworks to start. For most local stations, the cost of such a practice would be prohibitively expensive.

As a result, most local stations have used their access to the courtrooms sparingly. What they have taped and shown to their viewers is usually extremely inoffensive: shots of the judge entering the courtroom, or the defendant and his attorney sitting behind the defense table, or of the prosecutor addressing the court. These brief snippets have been used primarily as a visual backdrop to a reporter's account of developments in the trial. In most cases, little if any of the testimony of witnesses has actually been broadcast, and few if any of the arguments of either the prosecution or the defense attorneys.

In most of the jurisdictions in which television has been allowed into the courtroom, it has been accepted, at least temporarily. Judges, attorneys, jurors, defendants, witnesses and television viewers alike all seem to have gotten accustomed to its presence. Some still have deep doubts about the wisdom of televising trials, and some still strongly object to the practice, but most seem to have adjusted to it and learned to live with it, at least on an experimental basis.

The whole controversy might even have settled down, if not faded away altogether, were it not for the national televising of two notorious criminal trials. Both were the objects of national attention even before the decision to televise them was made, and both involved alleged acts of violence against women. In most other respects they were very different from each other, and the kinds of reactions they evoked from viewers across the country were different as well.

Their televising formed a stark contrast to the general rule of limited and noncontroversial broadcasting of trials. In these two cases, it was not just bits and pieces of the proceedings that were recorded and broadcast, but large portions or all of the entire trials. What's more, they weren't just broadcast locally, but nationally.

The enormous publicity they received rekindled the great debate on whether or not television should be allowed into the courts. Only this time the debate would not be primarily confined to members of the press and the judiciary. This time the debate, like the trials themselves, would be opened up to include much of the American public. Both sides would take their case to the public in newspaper and magazine articles and editorials. Most notably, television itself would devote many hours to the newly inflamed controversy.

Between them, the two trials would help to change the entire perspective on the old debate. They would raise new and important questions about the effects of televising trials—not just on the rights of defendants, the press and the public, but on the rights of witnesses and victims as well.

THE *VON BÜLOW* CASE

The first of these two historic trials was the trial, for attempted murder, of Claus von Bülow, which took place in early 1982. It was one of the most sensational trials of the twentieth century. Even the method of the alleged crime was an unusual one.

Claus von Bülow's wife, Sunny, had slipped into a coma at their mansion in Newport, Rhode Island on the night of December 20, 1980. It was a coma from which she has not emerged to this day. Claus was accused of having induced the coma in an effort to murder her by injecting her with an overdose of insulin.

Following the onset of the coma, several members of Sunny's family became suspicious of her husband. Searching for a black bag that belonged to Claus, Sunny's son (and Claus's stepson) Alexander von Auersperg found a closet in the Newport mansion locked. He hired a private detective and a locksmith and they went to the home and opened the closet. There was the black bag. Examining it, they found that it contained some drugs and a number of hypodermic needles. Alexander took them to a doctor, who had them tested. At least one of the needles had traces of insulin on it. In the doctor's opinion, considering Sunny von Bülow's medical condition, insulin could have caused her coma.

After a long investigation, Claus was eventually brought to trial. The case against him was mostly circumstantial, but it seemed strong. It was certainly scandalous. The motives alleged for the crime were love and greed. Although the von Bülows were wealthy, with a fortune measured in the tens of millions of dollars, most of the wealth came from Sunny. Claus himself, while well-off, was not a truly wealthy man. If Sunny died, he stood to inherit something like $14 million. The investigation suggested that Sunny had talked about a possible divorce, which would have left Claus considerably worse off. At the same time, it seemed that Claus had a girlfriend who had threatened to break off with him if he did not divorce his wife. Only through Sunny's death, the prosecution argued, could Claus hold on to both his girlfriend and his wealth.

The case had everything to recommend itself to television. Public interest in the case was enormous. It combined tragedy with mystery, and great wealth with family turmoil. It seemed almost like a real-life version of one of the prime-time soap operas (like *Dallas*), which were at that time among the most popular shows on television. It even went *Dallas* one better in terms of viewer interest. The von Bülows were not just tremendously wealthy, some of them were royalty. Before marrying Claus, Sunny had been married to an Austrian prince, Alfie von Auersperg, and her children by him, Alexander and Ala, still had claim to the titles of prince and princess.

An indication of the intense interest in the case was the flurry of requests from journalists for press credentials to the trial. It was so large that the trial was moved from Newport to Providence, Rhode Island, where a larger courtroom was available to hold the crush of newspeople. Among the requests were several from television journalists.

NATIONAL HOOKUP

At the time the *von Bülow* case came to trial, in January of 1982, the state of Rhode Island was in the midst of a one-year experiment with television in its courtrooms. A number of national television services, as well as the three local Newport television stations, were interested in broadcasting at least portions of the trial proceedings.

During the pretrial hearings, Harald Fahringer, one of Claus's attorneys, moved that television (as well as still cameras) be banned from the courtroom. His reasons for the motion were the likelihood that television would increase the notoriety of an already notorious case and the possibility that television would have an intimidating effect on witnesses, among other considerations. Justice Thomas H. Needham, the trial judge in the case, turned down Fahringer's request, ruling that television, under proper supervision, would be allowed.

It was decided that only one camera would be permitted into the courtroom itself. The three local stations would provide cameramen to run it on a rotating basis. The televised proceedings would be shown on a large monitor in a room in a building near the courthouse where members of the press could watch them. (Even the larger courtroom in Providence had proven too small to hold the crowd of national, and eventually international, journalists who wanted to attend the trial.) The television coverage of the trial, then, was not only a service to the public, but a service to the press itself. It allowed many more journalists to be "present" at the trial than could have attended otherwise.

Furthermore, through the rapidly advancing technology of television broadcasting, up to twelve separate television services (networks or stations) could be fed off that one large monitor. All twelve could then tape or broadcast the trial, in parts or as a whole, as each saw fit.

It was the first time that such an elaborate television hookup had been set up for a trial. It was also the first time that television coverage of a trial was made so widely available. The system was extended even further later on. Eventually signals were sent out from Providence that enabled any stations that wanted to, virtually anywhere in the continental United States, to broadcast portions of the trial to their viewers.

So it was that viewers across the country were able to share in important moments of the sensational trial. Most dramatic of all was the moment in which Claus von Bülow was found guilty of attempting to murder his wife and the jurors were polled, each standing to pronounce in his or her own voice the chilling word "guilty."

Some three years later, viewers were able to share in another, equally dramatic but very different moment in the *von Bülow* case. It came at the end of another long trial, brought about when the Supreme Court of the state of Rhode Island overturned the verdict in the original trial on state constitutional grounds and ordered that the case be tried again. The second trial was also televised. In it, certain questionable prosecution evidence that had been allowed in the first trial was disallowed, while the defense, led by a new attorney, Thomas Puccio, presented new medical testimony that indicated that Sunny von Bülow had not been injected with a coma-producing dose of insulin as argued by the state.

The television ratings for the trial were good. When asked, large numbers of viewers even proved willing to pay a price to assure that they would be able to watch. Midway through the trial, the cable television network CNN, which had been running almost gavel-to-gavel coverage, had second thoughts. They invited their viewers to call in and tell them whether they wanted the extensive coverage to continue. Each call cost the viewer fifty cents. Even so, the response in favor of continuing the coverage was so strong that CNN kept it up to the very end.

So it was that the second dramatic moment came about. As the television camera concentrated on the stoic face of Claus von Bülow, the foreman of the jury pronounced the words "Not guilty." Some five years after his wife had slipped into her coma, Claus von Bülow was finally a free man. He held a unique distinction. A national audience had watched him be first convicted and then acquitted of a terrible crime.

SURPRISING EFFECT

Comments on viewers' responses to the von Bülow trial have to come largely from speculation, since any scientific studies of these responses are lacking. But one response that seems to have been generated in at least some viewers of the televised trial came as a surprise to most observers. Against all predictions, the televising of portions of the trial seemed to arouse a great deal of sympathy for Claus von Bülow. This was particularly true in Rhode Island, where the trial took place and where it was followed with the greatest interest.

That response was surprising for two reasons. The first was the person of Claus von Bülow himself. Born in Denmark, von Bülow was, like Hauptmann, clearly a foreigner, a factor that might have been expected to count against him with the general public. He was a tall, thin man who wore expensively tailored suits as elegantly as a high-fashion male model. Even seen in miniature on a television screen, he exuded an aura of distinction, and also of aloof remoteness. Seen in close-up, his looks were striking. His forehead was impressive, and would have been considered high even if the front half of the skull above it had not been bald. His eyes were intelligent and firm. His facial features—a prominent chin, long nose, deep lines slashing down from each side of it to frame a broad, thin-lipped mouth—combined to give him an appearance that has been described as both handsome and reptilian. All in all, he looked every inch the European aristocrat many people assumed him to be.

His manner, as viewed on television, was calm and determinedly self-controlled. He sat so still in his chair behind the defense table that if his eyes had not been open it would have been hard to believe that he was awake. No evidence, however damning to his case, seemed to faze him. There was something unnatural about his presence, something distant and cold. He was not, it would seem, the sort of person the American viewing audience would be likely to identify with.

The other reason the sympathy for von Bülow was surprising was that it flew in the face of what had been the most widespread assumption about the effect of television in the courtroom. That assumption was that television was—or at least was most likely to be—prejudicial to the defendant.

Both Billie Sol Estes and the men in the *Chandler* case had appealed their convictions on the grounds that television's presence at their trials had resulted in prejudice against them. It was von Bülow's lawyers and not the prosecution who had wanted television banned from the courtroom in Providence. Von Bülow himself had given an interview in which he said that he feared that television would prejudice people against him.

And yet—despite his looks, despite the horrible crime with which he was charged, despite the assumption that television would stir up public feeling against him—there was a good deal of sympathy for Claus von Bülow. Pro–von Bülow crowds even demonstrated on his behalf outside the courtroom. A great many people, firm believers in his innocence, were appalled by the first verdict. (The verdict was overturned two years later by the Rhode Island Supreme Court on the ground, among others, that the black bag had been illegally seized and examined. None of the grounds had anything to do with television's presence at the trial, and in fact at his retrial, which began in spring 1985, television was once again allowed in.)

The sympathy for Claus, and the belief in his innocence, was far from universal. A great many other viewers of the trial were equally convinced that he was guilty. Further, there is no conclusive evidence that the televising of the trial was a major factor in generating sympathy for the defendant.

But one thing seems clear. Whether or not television helped produce support for Claus, the opposite effect, which virtually everyone expected television to have, never materialized. It clearly failed to arouse any widespread prejudice against him.

TRIAL IN FALL RIVER

The second of the two trials was even more lurid than the von Bülow trial had been, and it received even more extensive media coverage. In fact, both a local cable television service and at least one radio station carried extended portions of the trial live every day. Some sessions were actually carried gavel to gavel. The nationally seen cable service CNN (Cable News Network) carried hours of the trial each day to its millions of subscribers all across the country.

The trial that prompted all this media attention stemmed from a rape in the fishing community of New Bedford, Massachusetts. It came to be popularly known as the Big Dan's rape trial, after the tavern in which the crime had occurred.

Most rape cases do not generate the amount of interest generated in this case. The reason for the great interest this time lay not so much with the trial itself as with the first press reports (newspaper, radio, and television) that came out shortly after the crime occurred. Those reports announced that a woman had been sexually assaulted by several men in a public bar while a number of other male customers cheered the rapists on. The shock and outrage engendered by these reports assured the case of attention far outside the boundaries of Massachusetts. When Judge William Young, who presided in the case, decided that he would allow television to carry the trial, it became one of the most widely followed criminal trials in history. It was certainly the most watched.

Six men were charged in the case, four with physically participating in the sexual assault and two with encouraging the assaulters. All six pleaded innocent. They admitted that certain sexual activities had taken place in Big Dan's, but they claimed that the woman had been a willing participant and so there had been no rape.

As in the *von Bülow* case, only one camera was allowed in the courtroom. Judge William Young required that it remain stationary on one side of the courtroom, but permitted it to pan so that all parts of the courtroom could be seen.

One important restriction was put on what the camera could show. Because of the nature of the crime, and the fact that there was considerable emotional support for the defendants in New Bedford, the judge wanted to protect the alleged victim as much as possible. He ordered that the camera not photograph her, although it could be running while she testified.

The victim's testimony was the dramatic high point of the televised trial, even though she was never seen by the viewing audience. The prosecutor led her through a frightening story. She told how she had stopped at the bar to buy a pack of cigarettes. She'd stayed for a while to have a drink. At first the men in the bar had seemed friendly, but then they turned violent. Four of them had attacked her while others cheered.

When she was done, the defense attorney stepped forward for his cross-examination, and the viewing audience got a first-hand look at one of the most typical—and unpleasant—features of an American rape trial. Because the most important issue in a rape trial is often the question of whether the woman consented, the defense has to discredit her. Now, with the national audience watching on television, the defense attorney went on the attack. He berated the witness, attempting to prove that she was lying when she maintained that she had been attacked—that she had, in fact, encouraged the men, and only afterward claimed that she had been unwilling. He did everything he could, within the rules of cross-examination, to attack both her morals and her truthfulness.

The woman stood up bravely to the verbal assault, and ultimately it would become clear that the defense attorney had failed and that the jury believed her. But it was an emotionally exhausting confrontation. Even though the woman could not be seen, it was clear that she was going through a terrible ordeal, in some ways similar to the rape itself.

Eventually, after weeks of trial, the four men charged

with the actual physical assault were found guilty and sentenced to between six and twelve years in prison. The other two defendants were acquitted.

CONTROVERSIES

Feelings ran high throughout the trial, both within the courtroom and outside it. The case became a focal point for a feminist effort to educate the nation about the crime of rape. This was partly because of the early news reports about the cheering spectators (an aspect of the case left unsettled by the trial); but mostly it was due to the presence of television. Even before the trial began, three thousand women held a nighttime demonstration in New Bedford, marching with lighted candles in the dark streets. It made a dramatic picture for the television news.

All the attention, particularly from national television, troubled the community of New Bedford, especially the 60 percent of the population who were of Portuguese descent. All the defendants in the case were Portuguese (at least four of them were newcomers and still Portuguese nationals), and many felt that the media were slurring the Portuguese community with their massive coverage of the trial. Even though the victim, the prosecutor, and several of the jurors were also of Portuguese descent, many Portuguese-Americans felt that the trial was a kind of slander on their entire ethnic community. The result was a great deal of sympathy for the defendants and a corresponding hostility toward the victim among much of that community. Another result was a strong hostility against the press in New Bedford, particularly television, which many Portuguese-Americans accused of promoting the prejudice against them by increasing the notoriety of the trial.

All of this combined to make the trial enormously controversial. Much of the controversy centered on the press's role at the trial, particularly on the role played by television.

One major subject of controversy arose over use of the victim's name. Both the judge and much of the press were concerned with protecting her as much as possible from the hostility of the community, as well as the simple notoriety attached to being the alleged victim in a rape case. In such situations it is not uncommon for an understanding to be struck that the name of the victim should not be revealed by the press. That understanding had existed in the Big Dan's case. But on the very first day of the trial her name was used in the courtroom and was broadcast over the air. The television crew had not intended for it to happen, but they did not have the equipment on hand to bleep the name out. Once it had been broadcast, some newspapers printed it as well.

It may be that the victim's name would have been made public in some other manner anyway, but in any case the result of television's mistake was disastrous for her. The twenty-one-year-old mother of two little girls received death threats, as did her family. Things got so bad that she and her family were forced to leave New Bedford and take up residence somewhere else. (The location of their new home was not revealed.) It was widely agreed that if television is to cover future cases of a similar nature, it ought to have the facilities on hand to assure that such information will not slip out over the air.

There was still another controversy over the judge's effort to protect the victim. It had to do with his order that she not be shown on television. The attorneys for the defendants argued that his order was prejudicial. That is, they claimed that it showed special concern for the woman—a witness who, they claimed, was not telling the truth. By ordering her protected in that special way, they said, the judge was in effect telling the jury that she *was* a victim, that the rape had actually occurred, and that the defendants, therefore, must be guilty. Despite the defense's arguments, the judge held to his order and the victim was not shown. After the verdict, however, the defense announced that the issue would become a central element in their appeal of the four men's convictions.

Feminists, deeply concerned with the issue of rape and with the way that crime is handled by the courts, were of divided opinions about the televising of the trial. On the one hand, it had revealed to the public as nothing else could the graphic reality of a rape trial. It brought rape to the center of the national consciousness and made millions of people more sensitive to the issue than they had been before.

On the other hand, many of them were appalled at the sensational aspects of the television coverage. They felt that CNN had decided to carry the case not to inform the public about the horrors of rape but only to increase their ratings. It was distasteful to them that the increase in ratings should be accomplished at the cost of exposing the victim's ordeal to a massive television audience.

Judge Young regretted the mistake over the victim's name, but overall he was satisfied with his decision to allow the trial to be broadcast. He had made it to help inform the public, to "give them a sense of the trial process from beginning to end," and it had effectively accomplished that goal.

A RARE OPPORTUNITY

Both the von Bülow and Big Dan's trials were followed with intense interest by millions of Americans. It is impossible to say how much of this attention was due to the fact that they were televised and how much was simply due to the nature of the trials themselves. Certainly both cases had captured the public interest before the decision to allow them to be televised was ever made. But it seems likely that the interest was intensified by the ability of television viewers to actually witness the trials as they were taking place, to watch the participants, to judge for themselves the credibility of witnesses, and so forth.

The crimes alleged in these trials, attempted murder and rape, were serious offenses, yes, but the trials were historically significant events because of the fact that they were televised. They have a place in the histories of the American judicial system and of American journalism alike. Never before had so many Americans received such graphic and extensive lessons in the workings of the nation's criminal courts.

To what extent people took advantage of those lessons there is no way to tell. Television is today's dominant news and information medium. Like radio before it, it combines the two functions—disseminating news and providing entertainment—in intricate and sometimes confusing ways. Attempts are made to make the news entertaining, and to make the entertainment newsworthy. Both kinds of programming are advertised by stations and networks eager for viewers, and both are sponsored by businesses eager to attract customers.

There is some evidence in psychological studies that many viewers find it difficult to separate their emotional responses to television's two different functions. They may react to a fictional television drama as though it were a real event, and to a real event shown on the evening news as though it were a piece of fictional entertainment.

The dramatic aspects of a trial have already been mentioned. Many television melodramas have scenes involving trials in them, while the plots of some are entirely centered around the proceedings of a trial. At the same time, the outlines of the von Bülow and Big Dan's cases (more so than of most criminal cases) resembled the plots of television melodramas.

It is probable, then, that many of the viewers who tuned in to the trials responded to them in much the same way they would have responded to an ordinary television drama. They watched them for their entertainment value (enhanced, of course, by the knowledge that the trials were real) and didn't really think much about them at all.

But the televised trials were much more than ordinary television shows. The images on the screen were those of real people, whose private tragedies were being worked out before the viewers' eyes. What's more, the trial processes themselves were real. They provided thoughtful television viewers with much more than a few moments' diversion, however interesting. They provided viewers across the country with a rare opportunity to witness the American judicial system in action—an extraordinary and detailed experience of what has been called "the terrible majesty of the law."

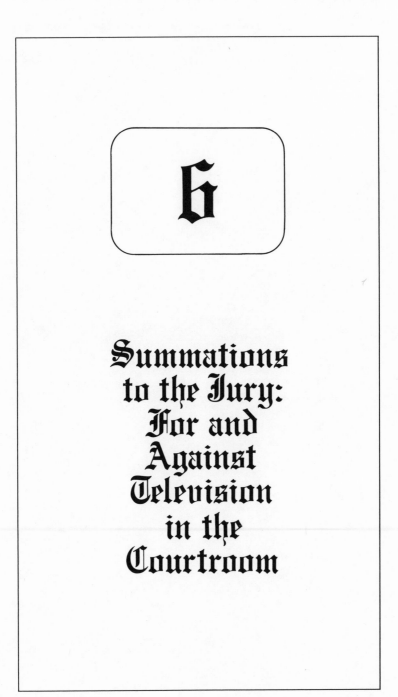

6

Summations to the Jury: For and Against Television in the Courtroom

THE CASE FOR
THE PROSECUTION

The arguments against the televising of trials can be divided into three categories: those dealing with possible disruptive effects on the trial itself, those dealing with negative effects on the reputations of people involved in the trial, and those dealing with the potentially destructive effects on the public's perception of the American judicial process.

Effects on the trial. Many of the arguments that fall into this category have changed little since the 1930s when they were first used against the use of radio microphones and movie and still cameras in the courtroom. As the opponents of allowing television into the courtroom see it, the presence of such technological equipment, plus the people needed to run it, is at the very least a distraction to the participants in a trial. At the worst, it is capable of destroying the legitimacy of the trial process.

A trial, in the phrase of Chief Judge Donald Lay of the U.S. Eighth Circuit Court of Appeals (a strong opponent of allowing trials to be televised), is a "solemn proceeding." It should be conducted in an atmosphere of calm deliberation. Everything should be done to promote the concentration of all concerned on the business at hand. The presence of a television camera works against that concentration.

Few people, argue the opponents, feel entirely comfortable in front of a television camera. As the well-known defense attorney Gerry Spence put it in an ABC television interview in which he, too, opposed televising trials: "A courtroom is a frightening place for everybody." The presence of a television camera only makes that fear more intense.

It is not merely a problem of psychological discomfort for the participants in a trial. The testimony of witnesses is likely to be negatively affected. Conscious of the fact that thousands (or perhaps millions) of people may be watching, a witness could be so flustered that he or she would forget important details, or remember them incorrectly. Worse, some witnesses may deliberately alter their testimony because of the presence of television. It is one thing to testify in a courtroom in front of a limited number of people, all of them in plain sight. It is another thing to testify in front of a vast, unseen television audience.

Testimony in a trial often involves making unpleasant admissions about your own conduct or circumstances. It is one thing to make such admissions to a small courtroom, but something else to make them, via television, to the whole world. Some witnesses might be unwilling to make such admissions knowing that their family, say, or their employer, might be watching them. The intimidating effect of television's presence may even mean that some witnesses would not come forward to testify at all.

Television, say its opponents, is likely to have quite another effect on many judges, prosecutors, and defense attorneys. Instead of intimidating them, it might spur them on to "grandstand" for the viewing audience. There could be many motives for this, even aside from the natural tendency some people have to play up to a large audience. Defense attorneys may try to show off in order to impress potential future clients. Many judges and prosecutors are elected officials. Knowing that the electorate is watching—the people who will either reelect them or throw them out of their jobs at the next election—they may be tempted to turn a trial into a campaign event.

Their judgment may be affected. If the community is concerned that the courts are being "soft" on criminals, for example, a judge who knows that he or she is being televised may be apt to give a harsher sentence than otherwise. On the other hand, if the television coverage seems to be generating public sympathy for the defendant (as it may have for von Bülow) the judge may feel it necessary to be more lenient.

The jury might be affected in a similar way. Knowing that their friends and neighbors are watching, the jury members could be influenced by their concerns about what those friends and neighbors might be thinking.

Juries might be influenced by television in another way as well. Most juries are not sequestered. When the proceedings are over for the day, the jurors simply go home. If they watch the nightly news and see the account of the trial there, they might be influenced by the way television presents the case. If a portion of testimony that they had not considered important was prominently featured on the television news, for example, they might be led to give it more weight in their own minds.

These concerns about television's effects on the participants in a trial are not frivolous. They go to the integrity of the trial process. Nor are they the concerns of only a small minority of observers. A 1979 survey of the members of the American Bar Association showed that fully three-quarters of all the attorneys who responded believed that television cameras would distract witnesses. Almost two-thirds thought that lawyers and judges would "grandstand" for the public watching at home.

Television's effects on reputations. The right to a "public" trial is guaranteed by the Constitution. That guarantee is made to assure that justice can be *seen* to be done. Without such a guarantee, there would be no way for the public to know that the courts are actually conducting trials according to the rules of due process. But while a "public" trial is a right, a televised trial may be an imposition.

The opponents of the practice argue that the mere fact that a trial is televised increases its notoriety. The public becomes more aware of it, and more deeply interested in it. More people—many of them far from the courtroom, or even far from the city and state in which the courtroom is located—become aware of the details of the charges and of damaging evidence brought out at the trial.

Inevitably, they also become more aware of the participants in the trial, and particularly of the defendant. The sight of a man or woman seated day after day behind the defense table in a courtroom etches the image of that person into the public consciousness. Even if the defendant is finally acquitted, that image of him or her as a person accused of a crime remains fixed in the public mind. There is no way to measure the full effects of the widespread prejudice that may result.

The witnesses at a trial, and even the victim of the crime for which the defendant is being tried, may suffer in much the same way. A trial, as we have seen, is an adversary proceeding. One element of this is the effort made by each side to discredit the witnesses for the other side. Sometimes they do this by bringing up witnesses of their own to testify that other witnesses were wrong— mistaken or even lying. Sometimes, as in the Big Dan's trial, they do it by harsh cross-examination, attempting to make the witness look confused, ignorant, foolish, or even corrupt. These practices are allowed to assure a fair trial. But when such attacks on witnesses are broadcast over television, a new element is added. The witness, who is usually only doing his or her civic duty by testifying, may now be held up to ridicule—or worse—in front of the whole community (in the case of a nationally televised trial, in front of the whole country). This is all the more unfair, say the critics, when the witness is the victim of a crime. In that case, the victim is victimized twice, first by the criminal and then by the publicity of the televised trial.

One result of all this, opponents claim, may be serious damage to the fight against crime. The televising of trials may actually deter victims and witnesses from coming forward at all. Without them, criminals are bound to remain free. This is not an idle argument, particularly when it comes to such emotionally charged crimes as rape. In the wake of the Big Dan's trial, a congressional committee held hearings. It heard testimony from rape victims who said that if the trials in which their rapists were tried had been televised, they never would have testified.

But, even in cases in which victims and witnesses are treated gently, the televising of trials can still adversely affect them. A certain stigma tends to attach in the public mind to anyone associated with something notorious, such as a heavily publicized criminal trial. Having that trial broadcast on television tends to increase that stigma and spread the notoriety more widely.

The effects on the public's perception of the courts. For many of the opponents of television in the courtroom, this category of arguments is the most important of all. This is because it is the most fundamental. As we have seen, faith in our judicial system is vital to the maintenance of our free society. But the net effect of allowing television to broadcast trials, say its opponents, will be to foster disrespect for the judicial system and eventually to cause the very loss of faith that must be avoided.

First of all, say the critics, only the most sensational trials would be telecast. That in itself would distort the public's perception of the court system, giving undue emphasis to such trials while ignoring the wide range of more mundane disputes that form the bulk of the courts' business.

If anyone should doubt that it would be the most sensational trials that would be broadcast, they only have to look at the record so far. The von Bülow and Big Dan's trials were not singled out for national telecasting at random. Television is a medium that seeks large numbers of viewers, and those trials were picked because their lurid and controversial aspects were likely to draw those viewers.

But whichever trials would be picked, televising them would necessarily distort them in the public's perception. That is because of the nature of television and of television viewing habits in this country. A trial is a complex thing. It unfolds over a period of time, and in the course of that time there are many developments. A case is made, piece by piece. It is then refuted, piece by piece. Only when the whole process has been gone through can a fair decision be reached. A juror sitting in the courtroom experiences the entire trial, hears all the testimony and all the arguments, sees all the evidence and is then able to come to an informed judgment. The same is not the case with the television viewer.

First of all, if past experience is any guide, the entire trial would rarely be televised. Television time is too valuable to devote whole days and even weeks to a single trial. But even if the whole trial were to be aired, few if any viewers would watch all of it. The nature of television viewers is such that most of them would turn the trial on and off at whim. They would only watch those parts of it they were particularly interested in, or that were scheduled conveniently for them. The end result would be much the same as if only portions of the trial had been telecast. Viewers would only have seen bits and pieces of the trial, and perhaps not the most important bits and pieces.

And yet, because of the nature of human psychology, most viewers would have the mistaken impression that they had, for all intents and purposes, "seen" the trial and understood what had taken place. This would be true even when they had, in fact, missed portions of the trial that were absolutely vital to any understanding of the outcome. A viewer might have seen and heard very damaging testimony to the defendant, but missed later testimony that completely disproved it. In such circumstances the viewer might well feel justified, if the verdict is "not guilty," in feeling that he or she had witnessed a travesty of justice. The viewer would be wrong, but the mere fact that trials are televised would be an invitation to this kind of misunderstanding, a misunderstanding whose ultimate effect is disrespect for the judicial process.

Perhaps the most damaging effect of televising trials, say the opponents of the practice, is that it will eventually result in equating them in the public mind with television entertainment programming. That equation, more than anything else, would lead to a loss of faith in the judicial system.

A trial, say the critics, may be entertaining, but it is not a piece of entertainment. It is not the equivalent of a game show, nor of a soap opera, and it should not be presented like one. A trial is a real event, in which the fates of real people are decided. It is a "solemn proceeding," as solemn and meaningful as anything in America's civic life. It should not be used to attract viewers for television advertisers; it should not be used as a form of light entertainment. To televise a trial for the amusement and titillation of television viewers—to interrupt it continually for commercials selling beer and toilet paper—is to demean the entire judicial process.

For all these reasons, say the critics, televising trials is a dangerous practice, one that not only threatens the rights of individuals to a fair trial, but threatens the judicial process itself.

THE CASE FOR
THE DEFENSE

Proponents of television in the courtroom argue that television must be allowed there except when a clear and compelling case can be made to keep it out. Just as in a criminal case the defendant is presumed to be innocent until proven guilty, television should be presumed to be acceptable until it can be proven—in a particular case— that its presence would cause serious prejudice or some other grave harm.

Some of television's supporters feel that such cases would virtually never arise. Others feel that they might be more common. (An example of such a case might be a trial involving crimes against very young children in which the children would be called to testify about psychologically troubling matters.) But all agree that the First and Sixth Amendments between them give the press the right to cover trials in any way they see fit, so long as they do not violate other constitutional rights in the process. They feel that the arguments made by television's opponents are largely overstated.

Effects on the trial. There is no proof, say the proponents, that television has any significant effect on the outcome of a trial. It is probably true that the presence of a television camera will make some participants nervous, but participants in a trial are inevitably nervous anyway. Any increase in tension brought about by television would be minimal.

A trial is a public event. Testimony is required to be given in open court, where both the defendant and the public can hear it. Television in no way alters that basic constitutional requirement. It simply makes it possible for more of the public to hear, and to judge, such testimony.

If judges and attorneys are tempted to "grandstand" for the camera, that is hardly the camera's fault. The answer to that problem is not to ban television, but to demand greater professionalism on the part of the judges and the attorneys.

It is also possible that the presence of television cameras may have the opposite effect on the officers of the court. Knowing that the public is watching, they may actually behave more carefully and judiciously.

As to the argument used by many defendants that television tends to bias the community against them, the evidence of the von Bülow trials (although it is far from conclusive) would seem to refute it. It may even point in the other direction entirely. It may well be that actually watching a defendant facing the ordeal of a trial prejudices much of the public in the defendant's favor.

When it comes to the opponents' fears that television may influence the jury, supporters claim that those fears are unfounded. Television is just one medium, and there is no reason to suppose that its coverage would have any more influence on a jury than that of any other medium. In extreme cases, juries can be sequestered. Even without such a drastic step, juries are routinely instructed not to read newspaper accounts of their trials and they can be instructed not to watch television accounts as well. Besides, television is going to report on trials whether or not its cameras are actually allowed into the courtroom.

Among those who argue that television does not affect the outcome of criminal trials is no less a figure than Judge William Young. He has said that in his extensive experience—which includes presiding over the most controversial televised trial to date, the Big Dan's case—television has not affected the way in which a trial was conducted, much less the final verdict.

Television's effects on reputations. Television's supporters maintain that this effect, too, is overstated. Television may make a person's face or name more widely known than it would have been otherwise, but the effect is only one of degree. To some extent, in fact, the effect is self-limiting. That is, only a trial that was already notorious would be widely broadcast and watched, and the important figures in such a trial would be widely known anyway. More ordinary trials, the participants of which might hope to escape public notoriety, would not be likely to be broadcast at all. If they were, they would not be widely watched. In any event, television is not responsible for whatever notoriety results from a person being involved in a criminal case. The notoriety comes from the circumstances of the case itself, not from the media, which only report on those circumstances.

Television's effects on the public's perception of the courts. In this area, television's proponents believe that the opponents have things backwards. Far from resulting in a loss of faith in the judicial system, televising trials could bring a rebirth of faith in the system. The public's perception of the courts, they argue, is already at a low ebb. The general public has the impression that the courts are too "soft" on criminals, don't care about the rights of the victims, and so forth. The best way to restore the good reputation of the courts is to let the public see what is really going on inside them. And the best way to do that is through television.

The public will see that the courts are not nearly as "soft" or unconcerned as they may think. At the same time, the problems that the courts *do* have will be openly revealed. This disclosure may lead to some disrespect at first, but it will also help lead to efforts to correct those problems. Ultimately, both the quality of the courts and the public's faith in them will be enhanced. In any case, it cannot be legitimate in a free and democratic society to argue that television should be kept out of the courtroom in order to hide from the public what is really happening there.

To the argument that television will necessarily distort the trials it covers by only showing parts of them, proponents respond that the argument is meaningless. Being exposed to a part of an important public event is surely preferable to not being exposed to any of it at all. Whatever distortion may occur because of the televising of a trial will be less than the distortion inevitable when all the public hears about a trial comes from the subjective interpretations of reporters on the scene. Whatever the extent of the televising of a trial, it will tend to add to the public's understanding of the case rather than to subtract from it.

As for the claim of opponents that television will demean the process by equating trials with ordinary television shows, proponents point out that that doesn't have to happen. The public is well accustomed to seeing both news and entertainment on television, and to say that the viewing audience is unable to tell the difference between the two is to underestimate them and insult their intelligence. If television can be used to broadcast presidential inaugurations and our first steps on the moon, among other important and even solemn events, there's no reason to assume that it will demean the trial process.

But the reasons given for allowing television into the criminal courts go far beyond these negatives. It is not just that there is not enough reason to keep it out. The televising of trials, say proponents, is not just a tolerable evil, it is a positive good. It benefits both the press and the public, and ultimately even the court system itself.

The press has the responsibility of informing us about the operations of our government, and that includes the operations of our courts. Television, say its supporters, is not merely a tool for fulfilling that responsibility, it is the best tool available. No other medium can give such a full, immediate and dramatic account of a criminal trial, taking the viewer inside the courtroom and letting him or her both see and hear exactly what is going on there.

Even more significantly, the televising of trials

informs us not just about the specific details of the particular trials being covered, but about the trial process itself. What's more, say the medium's proponents, the practice of televising trials allows the press to be objective in a way never possible before. Television can transmit the event to the public without bias, even, if it chooses, without selection or interpretation of any kind. It can give viewers the event whole, something no other medium has ever been able to do. Finally, it can allow the general public to see justice being done.

Another benefit of televising the criminal trial process, and one often overlooked by its critics, is its potential for deterring crime. Watching a criminal trial is a sobering experience. It is unlikely, say television's supporters, that anyone watched the verdicts being rendered in the Big Dan's case—and one of the defendants collapsing into tears—without a chill in the viewer's spine. It is even more unlikely that viewers watched the sentencing procedure televised in yet another case in which a young murderer was seen in a tense close-up hearing a judge pronounce his death sentence, without an actual shudder—as well as a much greater appreciation of the power and finality of the judicial process than they had had before.

Such views of the grim reality of the consequences of crime, say those who defend television's right to cover the criminal courtroom, may well be the greatest justification for its presence there.

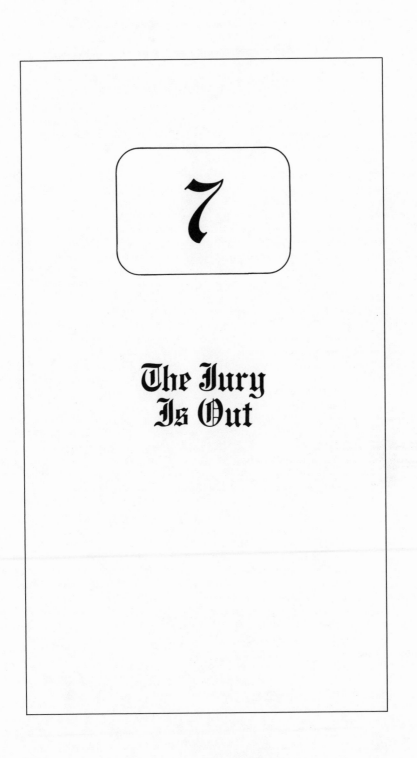

7

The Jury
Is Out

As of this writing, the jury is still out on the use of television and other modern journalistic technology in the nation's courtrooms. Cameras of all kinds, as well as all broadcasting equipment, radio or television, are still banned from the federal courts. The great majority of states, on the other hand, allow them into their courts under at least some circumstances.

In most of the rest of the world, however, the question—much less the technology—has hardly made it into court at all. This is surprisingly true of those countries whose legal systems are most closely related to our own: Great Britain (out of whose legal system our own evolved) and the other members of the British Commonwealth. In those countries, court proceedings are much more protected from the scrutiny of the press while they are taking place than they are here. It is considered contempt of court for any branch of the media to publish anything that might even "*tend*" to prejudice the public either against or for a criminal defendant in an ongoing case. Cameras and broadcasting equipment are resolutely banned, and there seems little likelihood that the ban will be lifted soon.

Interestingly, France, which forbids even a stenographic record being made of its criminal proceedings, may soon join the United States in experimenting with television coverage—although on an extremely limited basis. There is much interest there in the idea of televising the trial of the accused Nazi war criminal Klaus Barbie (known as "the butcher of Lyons") when it is held in Paris. If the trial is televised, however, it would probably be a one-time exception, made only because of the great national (and historic) interest in the Barbie case. It would be unlikely to establish a new rule allowing television coverage of ordinary criminal cases in France.

Here in the United States, though, it seems clear that over the long term things have been moving in the direction of more and more use of electronic journalistic technology in the criminal courts. In the short term, however, some observers feel that the enormous controversy surrounding the Big Dan's case may have been a setback, particularly for television. Still, no state seems inclined to reinstitute a ban on television as a result of it, and when the Claus von Bülow case was retried in Rhode Island, *after* the Big Dan's trial, television was once again allowed to broadcast it. The future of television in the state courts, then, looks promising. Its future in the federal courts is in much greater doubt.

In a country that honors democracy, it is often public opinion that decides public issues. If the public demands that the federal courts be opened up to modern media technology, they probably will be. It may well take a large surge of public opinion to overcome the federal judiciary's conservatism on this point, however, since that conservatism seems very ingrained. In that respect, it should be noted that a recent poll found only an indecisive 50 percent of the American public in favor of televising trials, with 38 percent opposed.

𝔅𝔦𝔟𝔩𝔦𝔬𝔤𝔯𝔞𝔭𝔥𝔶

No books focus on the specific subject of television in the courtroom, but a number of books deal with the more general subject of the overall relationship between the press and the courts. Among them are the following:

Gillmor, Donald M. *Free Press and Fair Trial.* Washington, D.C.: Public Affairs Press, 1966.

Reardon, Paul C., and Daniel, Clifton. *Fair Trial and Free Press.* Washington, D.C.: American Enterprise Institute for Policy Research, 1968.

The following book, while dealing with even broader issues concerning the media's role in society, contains an interesting chapter on the question of the press's rights and obligations in regard to the courts:

Marnell, William H. *The Right to Know—Media and the Common Good.* New York: The Seabury Press, 1973.

For anyone wishing to read Mr. Justice Clark's landmark opinion in the case of *Estes v. Texas*, along with Mr. Justice Stewart's dissenting opinion, they are reprinted in their entireties in:

Kahn, Frank J., ed. *Documents of American Broadcasting*. New York: Appleton-Century Crofts, 1968.

For those wanting more information on some of the specific criminal cases dealt with in this book, the following accounts will be of interest:

Ginger, Ray. *Six Days or Forever?* New York: Beacon Press, 1957. Deals with the Scopes trial.

Whipple, S. B. *The Trial of Bruno Richard Hauptmann*. Garden City, N.Y.: Doubleday, Doran & Co., 1937.

William Wright's *The Von Bülow Affair* (New York: Delacorte, 1983) is an interesting account of the von Bülow case, up to and including the first trial at which Claus von Bülow was convicted. However, it was written before the second trial and fails to take into account the powerful medical evidence that convinced the jury in that trial that the defendant was innocent and resulted in his ultimate acquittal.

Index